"It is exciting to me to read Christian scholars who take their faith and their discipline seriously. As a Christian and an anthropologist, Jenell Williams Paris does just that and applies her understanding to the challenging topic of sexual identity, drawing conclusions that, while controversial, warrant our attention and may lead the way to a more constructive conversation."

Mark A. Yarhouse, Psy.D., professor of psychology, and endowed chair and director of the Institute for the Study of Sexual Identity, Regent University

"Jenell Williams Paris brings a fresh perspective to the subject of sexual identity as she reminds us that we are all just people and far from perfect, 'each of whom is lover and loved.' She invites us to extend and receive grace even as she boldly encourages us to think a bit differently than we might about sexuality. I highly recommend it."

Lisa Graham McMinn, Ph.D., professor of sociology, and author of *Sexuality and Holy Longing*

"God gave us genitals, but he didn't stop there. He made us human. What does that mean? And what is love of neighbor? What is a welcoming church? What are strengths of celibacy when supported by Christian community? Not just scholarly but also painfully and hilariously personal, this book shatters stereotypes for the sake of the kingdom."

Miriam Adeney, professor, Seattle Pacific University, and author of *Kingdom Without Borders.*

"Jenell Paris does us a great favor by reminding us that God didn't create heterosexuals or homosexuals. People did, and fairly recently, in fact. Paris reveals the church's cultural captivity to Western ideas of sexual identity and orientation—that what we want, sexually speaking, is who we are. Humbug. Paris challenges the church with the words of Paul: don't be captive to the patterns of this world. Both heterosexuality and homosexuality—and the panoply of other possible identities and acronyms—are social constructions that pose problems for a people whose identity is to be found in Christ. Instead, Paris reminds us that God has redeemed us, called us by name and claimed us as his own. That is an identity worth affirming. Paris challenges us to live beyond sexual identity, even as we pursue sexual holiness, and provides us with a vision for what a post–sexual identity church might look like. This is a rich book, one that is long overdue. It is theologically sound, has deep ramifications for the church and will rattle some quarters. Good."

Mark D. Regnerus, professor of sociology, University of Texas, and author of *Forbidden Fruit* and *Premarital Sex in America*

"*The End of Sexual Identity* is a brilliant, bold, personal and biblically grounded work that is destined to become a classic in its field. By exposing the culturally conditioned nature of our modern Western 'sexual identity framework,' Paris completely reframes Christian debates about sexual ethics and thereby helps us (finally!) move effectively in our understanding of what it means to pursue sexual holiness. As a pastor, I have to confess that this is the most helpful, paradigm-changing and stimulating book on this topic I've ever read. I couldn't recommend it more strongly!"

Greg Boyd, senior pastor, Woodland Hills Church

"Jenell Paris has produced a provocative and astute diagnosis of our situation in the U.S.: living in 'an oversexualized culture with an undersexualized spirituality.' She refuses to argue in broad generalizations and to remain content with the polarized categories that Christian reflections on sex and sexuality so often produce. As a Christian cultural anthropologist she digs below the surface and brings a sophisticated interpretation of the cultural complexity of our sexual lives. Her most piercing contribution is in challenging the 'sexual identity framework' itself that traps both Christian and non-Christian reflection on sexuality. She exposes just how paralyzed Christians become by the categories borrowed from the cultural waters we swim in, particularly the socially constructed and historically recent categories of 'heterosexual' and 'homosexual.' Dr. Paris's insights will surprise and challenge readers from seemingly incompatible perspectives on these issues."

Jamie Gates, M.Div., Ph.D., cultural anthropologist and director of the Center for Justice and Reconciliation at Point Loma Nazarene University

"Honest. Smart. Provocative. Helpful. Important. Pitch-perfect. These are only a few of the words that came to mind when I read Jenell Williams Paris's book *The End of Sexual Identity*. This book is a must-read for engaging the issue of sexuality in our world today. Not only does Jenell call us to a better way to engage with sexuality, she casts a beautiful vision of what sexual wholeness and a post-sexual-identity church can be."

Doug Pagitt, pastor, Solomon's Porch, Minneapolis, Minnesota, and author of *A Christianity Worth Believing*

THE END OF
SEXUAL
IDENTITY

Why Sex Is Too Important
to Define Who We Are

Jenell Williams Paris

IVP Books

An imprint of InterVarsity Press
Downers Grove, Illinois

InterVarsity Press
P.O. Box 1400, Downers Grove, IL 60515-1426
World Wide Web: www.ivpress.com
E-mail: email@ivpress.com

InterVarsity Press® is the book-publishing division of InterVarsity Christian Fellowship/USA®, a movement of students and faculty active on campus at hundreds of universities, colleges and schools of nursing in the United States of America, and a member movement of the International Fellowship of Evangelical Students. For information about local and regional activities, write Public Relations Dept., InterVarsity Christian Fellowship/USA, 6400 Schroeder Rd., P.O. Box 7895, Madison, WI 53707-7895, or visit the IVCF website at <www.intervarsity.org>.

All Scripture quotations, unless otherwise indicated, are taken from the Holy Bible, Today's New International Version™ Copyright © 2001 by International Bible Society. All rights reserved.

While all the stories in this book are true, some names and identifying information have been changed to protect the privacy of the individuals involved.

Design: Cindy Kiple
Images: Image Source/Getty Images

ISBN 978-0-8308-3836-3

Printed in the United States of America ∞

 InterVarsity Press is committed to protecting the environment and to the responsible use of natural resources. As a member of Green Press Initiative we use recycled paper whenever possible. To learn more about the Green Press Initiative, visit <www. greenpressinitiative.org>.

Library of Congress Cataloging-in-Publication Data

Paris, Jenell Williams.
  The end of sexual identity: why sex is too important to define who
we are / Jenell Williams Paris.
    p. cm.
  Includes bibliographical references and index.
  ISBN 978-0-8308-3836-3 (pbk.: alk. paper)
  1. Sex—Religious aspects—Christianity. 2.
Homosexuality—Religious aspects—Christianity. 3. Identity
(Psychology)—Religious aspects—Christianity. I. Title.
  BT708.P36 2011
  261.8'357—dc22

                                                                2010040607

P   20   19   18   17   16   15   14   13   12   11   10   9   8   7   6   5   4   3   2   1
Y   27   26   25   24   23   22   21   20   19   18   17   16   15   14   13   12   11

Contents

Preface / 7

Introduction: *A Word About Sex* / 10

1 • WHAT IS DEFINED AS REAL / 23

2 • THE TROUBLE WITH HETEROSEXUALITY / 37

3 • THE TROUBLE WITH HOMOSEXUALITY / 55

4 • THE PROMISE OF SEXUAL HOLINESS / 77

5 • SEXUAL DESIRE IS (NOT) A BIG DEAL / 93

6 • HAVING SEX IS (NOT) A BIG DEAL / 111

7 • CELIBACY IS (NOT) A BIG DEAL / 125

Epilogue: *The End Is Near* / 139

Discussion Questions / 145

Notes / 149

Acknowledgments / 156

NAME AND SUBJECT INDEX / 158

SCRIPTURE INDEX / 160

123074

Preface

A few months into graduate school, a friend put me to the test: "I want to take you to a gay bar," Sarah challenged, "and see if you can handle it."

We had become close early in the semester but were beginning to see some deep differences between us. She was atheist, bisexual and a committed political progressive. I was heterosexual and evangelical, and my religion was far more important to me than my politics.

I accepted her challenge; after all, experiencing different cultural settings is what anthropologists live for. A group of us students rode the Metro to Washington, D.C.'s, Dupont Circle and went to a gay bar known to be fun for gay men, lesbians and straights. My friends knew I had just graduated from a Christian university, was raised in a very conservative home and had never been to a gay bar. I figured that made me different enough, so I didn't mention that I had never been to any bar at all.

As it turned out, I could handle being in a gay bar; I enjoyed being with my friends and wasn't shocked by anything I saw. At the same time, it was evident that I didn't know the music, didn't drink and just wasn't very cool. I felt like a fish out of water or, more to the point, like a conservative Christian out of church.

At one point, as a small group of us sat at a table, Sarah said, "Jenell, now that we're on my turf, let me ask you this: Does Christianity really condemn homosexuality?"

I blushed from being put on the spot but said what I believed to be true—that Christianity upholds sex only within marriage (which at that time was legally only between a man and a woman). With references to Leviticus and Romans, I explained my beliefs and claimed that I don't have the right to just revise centuries of Christian teachings. Endorsing sex only within marriage is what most Christians in most times and places have believed.

Sarah's face flushed too, but with anger. "I can't be friends with a homophobe," she barked. For the rest of our graduate studies we were cordial in class, but our friendship ended as quickly as it had begun.

I could see that my lesbian, gay and bisexual friends and classmates had interesting lives, wide-ranging intellects and compelling ethical perspectives. It seemed that my religion, on the other hand, had only one simplistic message: "Homosexuality is a sin." And it seemed that for me to be a good Christian, I'd need to repeat that message as often as possible. But the standard Christian line on homosexuality sounded like anything but good news. My friend felt judged by my response to her at the bar, and though I spoke in a measured (maybe even hesitant) tone, my words sounded judgmental to me too. I had stood up for my faith, so why did I feel like my faith had let me down?

Anthropology's focus on social construction—the human capacity (God-given, I believe) to create symbols, words, behaviors and ways of life together in societies—helped me begin to turn from a focus on judgment toward love. I continue to take my Christian faith as seriously as ever, but I've also learned to take the insights of cultural anthropology to heart. Now I can see that I described biblical teachings in a judgmental way because I had conformed to the pattern of the world—the sexual identity framework—and laid moral judgments on top of it. It's not that it was wrong of me to say that Christianity forbids same-sex sex; that just shouldn't have been the first and only thing I had to say.

There were so many things I didn't know then. I didn't know that sexual identity categories are social constructions, and that contemporary categories for sexuality weren't present in biblical cultures or even in my own society just over a hundred years ago. I didn't know that my heterosexuality was a problem; affiliating with a morally privileged identity category was limiting my humanity and my discipleship. And I didn't know that my sexuality is just as fraught as anyone else's. My friendship with Sarah ended, but through other relationships I learned to cultivate my Christian spirituality, sexuality included, in close friendship with people whose sexualities and sexual ethics are different than mine. In the process I learned that the journey toward sexual holiness is for all people and that no one has a head start, especially by virtue of feelings they didn't even choose.

In addition, I didn't know that proclaiming "homosexuality is a sin" is a poor representation of Christian teachings. I now see that statement as a judgment that served my needs. I needed to believe my religion was true, my sexual choices were proper, and my moral bearings were sound. Feeling unsteady in an unfamiliar environment, I stabilized myself by leaning on judgment instead of love. Now I realize that holiness is not synonymous with morality. Love and grace are not doled out according to our righteousness, but according to our belovedness. Jesus' good news should sound like good news, because it is.

It's been a long time since my gay bar challenge, and I wouldn't be surprised if Sarah has forgotten it. But I've been thinking about that disappointing encounter ever since. She and I would likely still disagree about sexual ethics, but I wish I could have a second chance to do my part in sustaining a dialogue and friendship with her. Instead of speaking for God so quickly, I wish I had introduced a pause in the rush to judgment. I could have said, "Tell me more about why you're interested in Christian perspectives." Or I could have said, "Wow, that's a loaded question. Let me share with you why I'm a Christian and how I think about sexuality in general." Or I could have said, "Can I have some time to reflect on your question?" And then, seventeen years later, I'd give her this book.

Introduction

A Word About Sex

Sex is much more than it used to be. Sexual desire is now considered central to human identity, and sexual self-expression is seen by many to be essential for healthy personhood. Media, public schools and medical professionals often teach that healthy adults, or even adolescents, should explore their erotic desires and express them in ways that feel self-fulfilling. The fact that sex is so important, and that sexual desire is seen as a central element of human identity, is new.

At the same time, sex is much less than it used to be. Sexual acts are often considered morally neutral, with no resulting shame or honor. We're told that sex can be mere recreation—unless a person *wants* it to be unitive or procreative or spiritual, in which case it can be that, if only for her or him. And sex is used for trivial purposes: to sell things, to gain attention, to build superstardom, to become popular or to write lyrics. These trivial reasons, along with more hearty purposes such as enjoying marriage or making babies, are often mixed together in people's personal sexual histories.

This discussion assumes, of course, a shared understanding of what sex is, but such a consensus no longer holds. Sex, like language, has become both much more and much less than it used to be. Theologian Bruce Hindmarsh complains that *spirituality* has become a "plastic" word, evoking positive feelings and associations but carrying no concrete definition—all ripple, no stone. Sexuality and spirituality are surely related in many ways; plasticity may be one of the less fortunate commonalities. What used to obviously be sex, such as orgasm by oral stimulation, now may or may not be, depending on your definition. And what used to be not-sex is now sex. Outercourse (what used to be called mutual masturbation or heavy petting), for example, is now promoted as a new form of sex that is "safe" because it doesn't result in pregnancy or disease.[1] Personal definitions of sex abound; for instance, if hand-holding or kissing is sexually intimate for people, then those acts may be sex, if only for them.

A student research project at a Christian college surveyed professors and students about their definitions of sex. The researchers asked whether oral sex counts as sex, and whether it breaches virginity. Most professors and students said oral sex is sex, though more professors than students believed this. Most professors, however, believed that virginity remains even after oral sex, while students were split: about half said virginity is lost, and half said it remains. It may be possible, then, to lose virginity without having intercourse, or to have sex and still be a virgin, depending on how you define the words.

Some Christians—Christians who probably hold a clear definition of sex—may view this as ridiculously complicated moral evasion. But these postmodern elements of language play and the elevation of sexual desire to an identity status raise legitimate questions for many about what sex is, what place it ought to have in human identity, and what sex ought to mean in Christian thought and practice. In a cultural anthropology class discussion on changing sexual practices in tribal Melanesia, one of my students asked, "To what degree are our sexual practices determined by our culture?" Another wondered, "Is it even possible to talk about same-sex relationships objectively in English? It almost seems like we need a new language." Even more than that, we need to keep our language, concepts and practices in an ongoing process of renewal that is simultaneously responsive to changes in society and faithful to our Christian commitments.

Sex Is (Not) a Big Deal

On the one hand, sex is a really big deal. It's essential for human reproduction and important for intimacy and relationship between lovers. It is also a source of great happiness and profound disappointment. Whether a person is sexually active or not, sexuality generates energy, creativity and beauty. It's a gift from God that we're invited to receive and enjoy.

Instead of enjoying sex as a good gift, however, Christians sometimes repress their sexual desires in an attempt to avoid sin or even try to ignore their sexuality altogether. Such Christians counter an oversexualized culture with an undersexualized spirituality. This distortion of purity depicts the good Christian as a disembodied spirit floating through this world on the way to heaven and portrays sex as something dangerous and dirty that ought to be kept in a darkened corner of life. Even when a person marries and sex suddenly becomes good and blessed, it is still kept in a corner, deemed to be a private and morally dangerous arena. This approach is an accident waiting to happen: what is repressed reappears, often in troubled form. Sex is a big deal and it deserves to be released from its darkened corner.

But on the other hand, sex is not a big deal, or at least not in the ways we're led to believe. On a personal level, we're told that our inner sexual feelings are the measure of our true selves—that by knowing, exploring and expressing our sexual desires, we become our real selves. Efforts to discipline or redirect sexual feelings for the sake of a greater cause may be seen as foolish or even dehumanizing. In the global economy, sex is bought and sold, and is used to sell other things, to gain happiness, to be beautiful and to achieve social status. When such a big deal is made of it, sex becomes an idol, offering identity and purpose to individuals and economic growth and international notoriety to nations. Sex is not such a big deal and it deserves to be dethroned.

It's time we put sex in its place, and that place is, well, our hands. You may or may not be making out, or making whoopee (as Bob Eubanks used to say on *The Newlywed Game*), but each of us should be making culture—specifically, sexual culture. We're responsible not only for what we do sexually, but for what we make of sex. In working together to make meanings and practices that demonstrate sexual wholeness and holiness in our time and place, we extend an invitation to acknowledge the myriad ways that sex is (not) a big deal.

A Word About Culture

Sexual holiness is often described as an unchanging ethic, universally applicable to Christians of all times and places, but it's not. Christians may agree that modesty, for instance, is an important virtue but differ widely as to how modesty ought to be practiced. One example: I often teach class dressed in Birkenstocks, a sleeveless shirt, and pants or a skirt with bare legs. I wear uncovered hair, gold or dangling earrings, and a little makeup. No one looks askance; it's fairly standard female-professor attire at my college. But to Christians of other times and places, nearly every element of my appearance would be considered immodest.

Even in my Christian circles, standards have changed. When I was a young Baptist churchgoer in the Midwest, pants or bare shoulders (especially in a church) communicated something negative about a girl's sexuality. Today those mean virtually nothing. In other Christian communities, gold jewelry or uncovered hair are still breaches of modesty. The principle of modesty may be stable across Christian communities, but its expression varies. Each local community of Christians works, ideally in dialogue with Christians of other times and places, to link up sex, gender, identity, desire and behavior in ways that are sensible, humanizing and holy.

New questions emerge with new generations, like what counts as having sex, when virginity is breached and what oral sex really means. If the problem were really just a matter of evaluating new sexual behaviors, however, it wouldn't be so difficult. Sexual identity is not just a new question, though; it's a new *kind* of question. The very notion that humans even have sexual identity is novel. People haven't always packaged up their sexual desires and behaviors into identity categories. Theology and ethics that focus on moral examination of sexual behaviors are still useful for that purpose, but applying these teachings to human identity is a different matter.

The task of this book is to do, on a larger scale, what I wish I had done in my conversation with Sarah: introduce a pause in the rush to judgment. Instead of quickly evaluating human identities the way we might evaluate behaviors, I want to cultivate a clearer perception of the current sexual identity framework. Then we'll consider how to foster Christian faithfulness in this sexual milieu, including stewardship of one's own sexuality as well as how to evaluate other sexual identities. This can be uncomfortable, difficult and even contentious at times, but ultimately, making good culture is worth the effort.

A Word About Patterns

As we think about sexual identity and culture, Paul offers us some important words in Romans 12, particularly in verses 1-2:

> Therefore, I urge you, brothers and sisters, in view of God's mercy, to offer your bodies as a living sacrifice, holy and pleasing to God—this is true worship. Do not conform to the pattern of this world, but be transformed by the renewing of your mind. Then you will be able to test and approve what

God's will is—his good, pleasing and perfect will. (Romans 12:1-2)

Based on their pre-Christian practices, Jewish believers would have appreciated the importance of offering acceptable sacrifices to God. Paul pushes the metaphor to say that the believers' very selves could be acceptable sacrifices, not by killing or shedding blood, but by the way they live. Furthermore, in contrast to forms of worship and philosophy that emphasized ecstatic worship or formal ritual, Paul highlights the importance of thinking rightly. A "living sacrifice" is a life in which a person does not just live out of unthinking conformity to the pattern of the world but is renewed in the mind, which leads to loving, discerning life in community.[2]

As an anthropologist, I'm inspired by Paul's words because cultural anthropology is devoted to understanding the patterns of the world: ways of life that people cultivate, share with others and pass on to future generations. As a Christian anthropologist, I use my academic study as a spiritual discipline, trusting God to renew my perspective in ways that can make my life (not just my studies) a living sacrifice.

Romans 12 also inspires the structure for this book. Chapters one, two and three describe the way sexuality is patterned in our world. Like many anthropologists have already done, I describe heterosexuality and homosexuality as social constructions. Though these categories claim to be natural, neutral descriptions of human beings, they are actually concepts created by people within the last two hundred years. When Christians develop theology and ethics about homosexuality and heterosexuality, then, they are really evaluating elements of culture, though they often mistakenly believe sexual identity as we know it today was given by God at creation. Chapter one describes the social construction of sexual identity, both what that phrase means and how social construction happens. Chapter two deconstructs heterosexuality, suggesting that heterosexuals may have a plank in the eye that's been neglected. And then chapter three describes how concepts such as homosexual, lesbian, and gay have developed over time. These chapters analyze sexual identity in a way that reduces the moral hierarchy of heterosexuality over homosexuality, and invite each of us to consider stewardship of sexuality as an important part of Christian discipleship.

This work of learning to perceive our enculturation—the ways we were taught to live in a particular culture—is like turning our eyes around and looking into our own heads. This sounds uncomfortable, and it is. Taken far enough, our own identities, the nature of the world around us and even our understandings of God may begin to feel unsteady. I intend to go that far, not to be destructive but to really see the patterns of the world to which we ought not conform. Romans 12 speaks to more than just movies, swear words or behaviors that are sinful and should be avoided, going much deeper to consider how our minds and lives are patterned by culture.

Building on the foundations of the first three chapters, chapter four describes the promise of sexual holiness, a contemporary adaptation of a time-honored Christian virtue. What might it mean to live after the end of sexual identity? A post–sexual identity church will reconfigure human sexuality, making meaning of sexual desire and behavior in new ways.

Chapters five, six and seven play out the implications of sexual holiness for various aspects of sexuality. Chapter five examines the meaning of sexual desire, arguing that it should not constitute human identity as it currently does for both heterosexuals and homosexuals. Chapter six is about being sexually active: why it's so important, and why it's not really so important. Chapter seven addresses the same concerns, but about celibacy. In the end, readers will be invited to a fresh perspective on their own sexuality, and will be encouraged to engage diverse sexual views in the church with respect.

A Word About Cultural Anthropology

Cultural anthropology is the description and interpretation of similarities and differences in human cultures. Anthropologists use library research, laboratory work and detached observation as needed, but the heart of our approach is participant-observation, full immersion in other ways of life. This is what drew me to anthropology—its incarnational nature. Anthropologists learn by deeply involving themselves in the everyday lives of the people they are studying, sometimes for several years at a time.

I became an anthropologist out of my commitment to urban ministry, specifically. After a summer of short-term mission in a Philadelphia neighborhood, I came back to college wanting to learn more about reducing poverty. I had a lifetime of Bible education and church experience and was majoring in biblical studies, but I knew virtually nothing about poverty, race or cities. I therefore changed my major to sociocultural studies and focused in anthropology so I could integrate my faith with social science insights about social inequality. When I left the biblical studies major, my academic adviser warned me that studying anthropology could make me "liberal." The truth of the matter (which I was glad to learn) is that many Christians in anthropology apply their academic understandings to Bible translation and missions as well as to helping churches engage cultural differences. Others, like me, study subjects that aren't directly related to religion (like urban poverty or sexuality), and integrate anthropology and Christianity in a variety of ways.

Human sexuality and urban ministry are not so different in terms of how an anthropological perspective benefits Christian understanding. By understanding how poverty is patterned and perpetuated through economic and political systems, I became more discerning about how to positively influence urban neighborhoods. Similarly, by learning about the vast variety of ways that humans live, including in their sexualities, I can be more thoughtful about what sexual holiness may mean in my own social context.

Christianity and anthropology also harmonize in their high view of ethics and respectful treatment of others. The American Anthropological Association's Code of Ethics requires us anthropologists to honor, above all, the people we study. Anthropologists must "do everything in their power to ensure that their research does not harm the safety, dignity, or privacy of the people with whom they work, conduct research, or perform other professional activities."[3] Really, it's harmonious with the golden rule, treating others as we would like to be treated.

Stories in this book are mostly about people I've known personally or professionally, and others I've read about. To protect the privacy of individuals, I have changed identifying details; people in these stories are identified by pseudonyms. When stories are from published sources and are part of the public record, I use real full names and cite sources. If I quote a student's writing, it is always with permission, even with a pseudonym.

A Word About Me

The mission statement of Messiah College, where I teach, states that the college "is committed to an embracing evangelical spirit," a phrase I like to borrow in describing my own spirituality. Evangelicalism is both my tradition of birth and my tradition of choice. I was carried in utero to Sunday morning worship and Wednesday evening prayer and have continued good attendance through the present. Like many evangelicals, my denominational loyalty is relatively weak, so churches I've attended include Baptist, Evangelical Covenant, Evangelical Free and Church of God (Anderson, Indiana). For six years I was a covenant participant at Solomon's Porch, a church in Minneapolis associated with the emergent movement. Now I live outside Harrisburg, Pennsylvania, and my family attends a Brethren in Christ church.

I attended a Christian university (Bethel University '94), and from the time I graduated through my early thirties lived in low-income neighborhoods in Philadelphia, Washington, D.C., Buffalo and Minneapolis, serving with urban ministries and studying urban anthropology both during and after graduate school. I've spent my entire career teaching at Christian colleges: the Council for Christian Colleges and Universities American Studies Program, Bethel University and now Messiah College.

During graduate school my aspirations focused on becoming a Christian college professor, but I gave myself one big warning: if you become a professional Christian (employed by a Christian institution), you better not be nice. Niceness is not a biblical virtue; in fact, I consider it a vice. Nice Christians pretend things are fine when they're not, say one thing and do another, and avoid difficult conversations. Niceness is rampant among Christians and it does damage. The real virtues of our faith such as honesty, love, discipleship, repentance and reconciliation require looking life full in the face and speaking the truth in love as best we can. Now that I am a professor, I try to be a safe person for students who want to talk about sex, either in their worldview or in their relationships. "Safe" doesn't mean that I always say what they want to hear, though. I simply try to listen to their stories without judgment and without causing shame and respond as best I can. In doing so, I encourage them to face God for themselves, claim and tell their own stories, and continually try to match their behaviors with their beliefs.

This book is written in the same spirit with which I do my work. I critique American Christianity, especially evangelicalism, but only because I care so much. (When I was the one getting spanked, that phrase always sounded lame. Now I guess I see what my parents meant!) It's my contribution to getting my own house (my religious tradition) in order. That means saying some uncomfortable things, exposing some awkward truths, and acknowledging questions and conundrums that don't easily resolve. While to some that may seem like a lack of faith, for me it is an expression of faith. In this I'm not even necessarily trying to win everyone over to my views. What I am trying to do is open up a conversation about culture and spark new ways of framing issues we've been looking at for some time.

I should also add that I am a wife and a mother. My husband, James, and I are in over our heads caring for our three boys: preschool twins and a toddler. My life stage and family commitments shape my views on sexuality, and you'll see that influence throughout the book.

Words of Warning and Reassurance

A forewarning about sexual content in this book: there will be some. Please be assured that I don't use potentially offensive words or stories gratuitously, and I understand it is challenging for some. I like to think of myself as one who is not easily shocked, but sometimes even my boundaries get pushed. This happened recently at a conference, hosted by Point Loma Nazarene University in San Diego, where I was a panel respondent following Jean Kilbourne's "Killing Us Softly" talk about how advertising negatively shapes relationships between men and women.[4] Delivered to an auditorium full of Christian college students, professors and administrators, her presentation was filled with images from fashion magazines of semi-nudity, sexual acts, sexualized images of children and sexual violence, and her commentary was equally frank. At first I was surprised that such a talk was hosted by a Christian college, having never seen the likes of it in all my years in Christian higher education, but then I was even more surprised by student responses. There was a time when students would have stood up for their faith by, literally, standing up and walking out. But in this situation, they murmured and gasped in disapproval at the bad parts, laughed at the speaker's jokes, participated in the public Q&A, and stood in line afterward to ask her questions.

Standing up for faith in an oversexualized culture doesn't only mean averting our gaze. It can mean thoughtful engagement, even respectful face-to-face dialogue with people we disagree with. Jean Kilbourne's talk also reminded me that today's young adults have been socialized to accept more sexual content than those of us raised just a decade or two before. There are downsides to this, to be sure, but one advantage is that we can be full participants in our world, culture makers (to borrow a phrase from Andy Crouch) and not just sideline judges.[5]

So consider yourself warned. Sexuality is a touchy subject, both literally and intellectually, and I won't pretend otherwise. But be reassured: throughout the book I use my Christian college class-room as a point of reference; whatever I discuss in this book, I would also discuss—and probably have—in class.

A Word About Respect

Christian scholar Harold Heie gave an address at Messiah College titled "Respectful Conversation."[6] He critiqued the fixed-position model of dialogue that we see on TV talk shows, in political dialogue, and often in the church and academy as well, in which positions are preset and inflexible. In this model, people seek validation of positions they already hold and are closed to new perspectives or real learning. Heie said moving beyond fixed positions can be difficult for Christians because it may seem that the alternative is a "whatever" kind of relativism, just listening to others for the sake of listening, or considering all options equally valid. He urged Christian colleges to model a third way beyond the unacceptable extremes of fixed positions and relativism. Respectful conversation includes personal, face-to-face dialogue between people who disagree. It invites risk-taking, not just posturing, making yourself and your views vulnerable in encounters with others, anticipating growth and learning.

One formative experience from my high school days illustrates why I too want to promote respectful conversation in faith communities. At a church youth gathering, a leader said French kissing was a sin. It was moral to kiss with a peck, hold hands or hug goodnight, he told us, but anything more was a sin.

I went to him privately and said, "But I *have* French kissed. More than one boy. And I don't feel convicted about it. Am I so deep in sin that my conscience is no longer pricked?"

He said, "I just said that to the group to try to prevent people from going too far. In my personal opinion, French kissing isn't a sin, but it can lead to sin, so it's better to err on the side of restraint."

As an adult, I can appreciate his attempt to balance grace and discipline, but at the time it seemed like hypocrisy. That was the first time, but by no means the last or the most egregious, that I saw evangelicals squirming and even losing their bearings altogether around sexual issues. Among Christians, including pastors, I have seen pornography abuse, pedophilia, adultery, solicitation of sex workers and boundary-flirting relationships with young parishioners, and those are just from the handful of churches I've attended. There are plenty more examples from high-profile Christian leaders whose discretions hit the national media.

The point is that we're kidding ourselves if we think Christians have sex figured out. Reticence to engage the issues in a sustained and civil manner has led—and is still leading—to secrecy, repression, taboo and scandal. We need to treat everyone, fellow believers and all other humans as well, with respect as we try on new ideas, test them out, refine them and learn together.

What Is Defined as Real

My sons love to ask questions. When they were ages four, four and three, some of their favorite questions were about their bodies. One evening during bath time, I was tripped up by two good ones: "What's inside my fingernail?" and "Mommy, can you take off my foot so I can see the bones inside?"

I stumbled in a different way over this one: "Mommy, what are these?"

"Testicles," I said.

"What are testicles?"

"They are part of what makes you a boy," I said. "All boys have testicles." Immediately I felt disappointed with myself. "All" was a poor word choice. A boy who loses one or both testicles to accident or disease is still a boy. Some intersexual people are born with both testicles and ovaries. And in the Dominican Republic, due to a genetic issue, a number of children (called *guevedoces,* which means "balls at twelve") were raised as girls, but then at puberty their testicles descended, and most (but not all) shifted to become boys.

One of my favorite quotes, taped to my office door, is, "What is defined as real is real in its effects."[1] It may not be true that all boys have testicles, but if my sons take it as truth, there will be real consequences. Defining boyhood as strictly as I did would rule out the exceptional cases and might cause a son to question his own maleness should he lose one or both testicles.

Before I had a chance to launch into a college-level lecture from my perch on the bathroom sink, one boy announced, "Then baby boys don't have testicles."

Another said, "And neither do mommies or daddies or bears."

"All" caused another problem. In their minds, because all boys have testicles, baby boys, mommies, daddies and bears are in the category of "those without testicles." At their developmental level, they're learning to identify males and females. They need to understand that baby boys, boys, men and daddies are all male, just as baby girls, girls, women and mommies are all female, and that animals like bears come in male and female varieties. They also need to understand that every category has complications and exceptions, but that will be a conversation for later.

I stand by my claim that testicles are part of what makes a boy a boy, but I wish I had stopped there. By claiming that *all* boys have testicles, I made the category too rigid and didn't leave room for other ways of seeing boys, and for other kinds of boys. Depending on the context, "boy" could be defined genetically in terms of chromosomes (in a science class), biologically in terms of anatomy (at home in the tub) or even socially in terms of self-presentation (if a transgender girl passes as a boy, then socially she is a boy). Creating categories, even one as seemingly simple as "boy," is not just descriptive. Categories also prescribe what is normal and right, and who belongs and who doesn't.

Like the categories of male and female or boy and girl, human sexuality is part of culture. Sex is a gift from God, but we don't receive it straight from heaven; it is always mediated by culture. We learn from others how to be sexy, how to find a sexual partner, and even which sexual behaviors are possible, desirable or typical. We can't even speak about sex without culture, as language provides shared symbols that enable communication. Consider common English phrases for sexual intercourse. "Having sex" emphasizes sex as a thing that is possessed by individuals. "Doing it" portrays sex as an action performed by individuals, with "it" inferring that sex is something mundane or ordinary. "Making love" highlights intimacy and romance, and also seems to correspond with an industrial economy in which producing goods and services is valued. Taken together, contemporary ways of speaking about sex encourage people to think of sex as something an individual can have, get, make or do. More graphic euphemisms portray sex as dirty, naughty or meaningless. Language reflects the cultural meanings ascribed to sex, which shape how people express sexuality. It's true: what is defined as real is real in its effects.

There are many cultural dimensions of human sexuality, and sexual identity is an important one. Sexual identity is a cultural pattern by which people understand their sexuality. It's a concept that was created by people in an attempt to conceptualize human sexuality more clearly, and it has become a shared understanding that is passed on to others. In his letter to the Romans, Paul's immediate focus was on broader issues of life in the church in Rome, but studying the sexual patterns of the world is a fitting response to his appeal in Romans 12 to cultivate reasonable or rational worship.

The Familiar Strange and the Strange Familiar

Sex seems so biological and so natural that you might assume sex works pretty much the same way for all people. But the anthropological perspective reveals that what seems "natural" may or may not be from nature. It may seem perfectly normal to eat cereal for breakfast or to sleep indoors, for example, but a cross-cultural perspective would reveal that those habits are not a natural part of being human. Other people have practices that seem just as normal to them. So while it may seem perfectly natural to date before marriage, or to have sex in a bed, or to kiss in public (or to never kiss in public), none of these practices are cultural universals.

People often find that when they are immersed in a different culture, what is initially strange becomes familiar, and what was once familiar begins to seem strange. Experience in other cultures can help open our eyes to the uniqueness of what we take as "just normal" in our own world. Through long-term immersion, anthropologists try to understand the insiders' view of other cultures. Sharyn Graham Davies, an Australian anthropologist, spent nearly two years living in South Sulawesi, a small region of Indonesia, among the Bugis ethnic group.[2] She immersed herself in the everyday lives of men, women, *calalai*, *calabai* and *bissu* (the five gender categories in their society) with the goal of understanding, in part, how Bugis gender roles relate to people's sexualities.

The Bugis blend of indigenous tradition and Islam, the national religion, leads them to believe that people can embody different amounts of maleness or femaleness, which allows for the possibility of more than two genders.[3] Instead of separating men and women into discrete categories, imagine a line spanning from man to woman. *Calalai* (masculine women) are born female but have so much male essence that they live as men in that they travel, dress as men and work in men's professions; sometimes they are even mistaken for men. *Calabai* (feminine men) are born male, but their extra female essence leads them to dress and act as women, but in an over-the-top, glamorous, sexy way. They don't feel they are women trapped in a man's body; they feel they are *calabai*, feminine males. *Bissu* (transgender shamans) are the perfect combination of female and male elements, having come to earth from the spirit world without being divided into male or female. This is reflected in the body; many *bissu* are intersex, that is, born with ambiguous sexual biology. This is believed to animate their spiritual power, which is used to bless important life events like birth, marriage and death.

The overwhelming majority of Bugis people are men or women, but the notion of gender as a spectrum from male to female, and an emphasis on gender identity as shaping social roles (contrasted with our society's focus on sexual identity), makes room for *calalai, calabai* or *bissu* to find tolerance or even acclaim in their local communities. It also shapes men's and women's sense of themselves as existing on a continuum, not as "opposite" sexes, or as different as Mars and Venus.

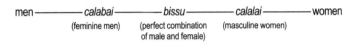

men ——————— *calabai* ——————— *bissu* ——————— *calalai* ——————— women
      (feminine men)   (perfect combination   (masculine women)
                         of male and female)

Figure 1.1. Five Bugis genders

For traditional Bugis, it would be unthinkable to be gay or lesbian. Identities based on sexual feelings are not present in their culture. Sexuality provides confirmation of gender identity (a *calabai* who desires women, for instance, may be suspected of being a fake), but people don't form identities or communities around sexuality in and of itself.

Limited Imaginations

Contemporary Christian dialogue about sexuality is limited because it is framed by contemporary Western notions of sexual identity. It seems virtually impossible to find fresh ways to move forward when our imaginations are bound by the culture that shaped them. For example, Christians often become absorbed in either affirming or negating the morality of same-sex sex and related issues such as ordination of gay and lesbians and same-sex marriage. While these issues certainly are important, we must also address the underlying problem that drives these disputes. These "fixed position" debates are binary: first, framing the issue in terms of homosexuality and heterosexuality, and then asking for only affirmation or negation of same-sex sex, without more complex dialogue about human sexuality and Christian discipleship.

Because of the cultural distance, it may be easier to see how the

Bugis five-gender paradigm leads to opportunities and problems that are distinctively Bugis than it is to see how our paradigms frame and direct our concerns. Imagine a child born with ambiguous genitals who grows up to display special spiritual interest and abilities. If you were Bugis, you'd identify this child as a potential *bissu*. If you were North American, you might never know this child as intersex because she or he would likely have had medical intervention in early childhood and be living as a girl or boy. Furthermore, if an intersex child showed special spiritual interests and abilities, the North American imagination wouldn't connect spiritual traits with sexual physiology.

Now imagine a boy with enduring sexual feelings for other boys, but with otherwise masculine interests (no inclination to dress or act in feminine ways). If you were American, you might think he's gay. If you were Bugis, you wouldn't know what to make of him; there would be no category for him. The boy would likely be encouraged to marry and have children, which is necessary for full citizenship. Sexual desires that transgress marriage would have to be stifled, or indulged in violation of religious and community norms.

As far as I have read, there are no Christian theologies of Bugis sex and gender. But if there were a Bugis Christian congregation or seminary that wished to pursue these issues, believers would benefit from perceiving the socially constructed nature of *calalai, calabai, bissu,* and even their understanding of *man* and *woman*. Most Bugis are Muslim, and they have a variety of responses to the indigenous five-gender system. The *bissu* role is of central concern because it involves spirituality and religious ritual. Some Muslim Bugis reject the *bissu* role altogether because it is not strictly Muslim. Others see Islam as "religion" and *bissu* rituals as "culture," and therefore protect the *bissu* role in the name of preserving Indonesian indigenous cultures. Some *bissu* who are also Muslim have replaced the pre-Islamic gods of their rituals with Allah. Whether or not it is explicit, these approaches acknowledge that sex and gender variations cannot be understood as solely moral dimensions of life; they are embedded in cultural beliefs, mixes of local culture with national religion, and available technologies (lack of surgeries for intersex babies, for example).

It's almost always easier for an outsider to see the socially constructed nature of beliefs, concepts and practices; to an insider, their way of life is not just one of many possible worlds—it is just *the* world. It's much more difficult for us to see how culture shapes our own beliefs and practices, but we aren't as different from the Bugis as it may seem. Christian theology about homosexuality, for example, borrows that sexual identity category from American culture and then interprets and evaluates it with Scripture (which was written in various cultural contexts), and with Christian theology from various places and times. We might like to believe that religion and culture are as separate as meat, potatoes and vegetables on a picky child's plate, but that's impossible. Culture provides the words, practices, sounds, buildings, musical instruments and so on, with which we make our religious lives.

Because they configure sex and gender differently, the Bugis help me see that believing in social identities linked directly to sexual desire is just that—a belief. Cultures link sexual feelings, biology of birth, gender roles, work, dress and marital roles in various ways. Other societies, including those described in Scripture, can be both windows and mirrors: windows that offer glimpses into other ways of life, and mirrors that help us see ourselves more clearly. The Bugis conform to the pattern of their world, and U.S. Americans to the pattern of ours. The very word *culture* highlights the way people cohere into a functioning society with a shared language and way of life. That's a good thing—the capacity to make culture is a God-given gift that strengthens human survival—but as believers we're called to be discerning about the ways we participate in, carry forward and transform our cultures.

Seeing the Matrix

I warned them it was going to be postmodern. It was an upper-level anthropology seminar on sexuality in crosscultural perspective, a challenging topic at a Christian college, and the students said they were up for it. First things first: define homosexuality and heterosexuality. "We all know what we're talking about here, right?" I teased. "So this should be easy." Students wrote definitions on the board about attractions, feelings and behaviors, but no one seemed enthusiastic about the answers; in discussion they offered some real-life examples that didn't seem to fit the categories. Consider a faithfully and happily married man who has occasional same-sex temptations. He calls himself heterosexual, but is he really? Or a woman who, after years of same-sex relationships, marries a man. Was she really homosexual? Is she now heterosexual?

Michael spoke up, "I'm not so sure I'm straight. Don't get me wrong—I'm not gay, and my girlfriend hates it when I talk like this—but really, are these my only choices? I'm a whole person, with a multifaceted history and a complicated identity, and to just reduce all that to 'gay' or 'straight,' well, it just doesn't fit me very well." Some classmates resonated with him immediately, and one asked clarifying questions just to be sure Michael really wasn't gay. Others expressed disappointment at how easy it was to dismantle straightness; it's an important element of identity, and they expected it to be sturdier.

Sexual identity is extremely important to many, and people expend great effort shaping others' perceptions of them as gay, straight, bisexual or some other designator. For example, my friend's son, around age ten, was called "gay" because he wasn't very competitive in sports at school. He had never been in a fight before but picked a fight with another boy just to prove he wasn't gay. Crises of faith, identity and family emerge when people shift categories, or feel their inner experience is incongruent with the sex or gender label given to them at birth, or are unable to persuade others to see them in their desired category. But try to define "gay" or "straight," and the words begin to slip through our fingers. Those concepts may have better described sexuality in Western societies at the time they were created (the subject of the next chapter), but using them today often feels like squeezing feet into ill-fitting shoes.

Michael told us that his sister had recently come out as a lesbian and that his Christian family was struggling with it. He was very close to his sister and was pained by how her coming out separated them into two different types of humans. She wasn't making that happen and neither was he, but the words and concepts available for understanding sexuality just somehow built a huge separation between them. When Michael said, "I'm not so sure I'm straight," he wasn't questioning his sexual identity in the conventional meaning of the phrase. He was saying he's dissatisfied with his inheritance, culturally speaking. Making sense of his sexuality, or his sister's, in terms of currently available social categories just wasn't good enough; he saw the matrix and wanted something better.

The Social Construction of Everything?

In contrast to socially constructed concepts like *calalai* or *homosexuality,* categories such as *male* and *female* seem more valid. Sex is often contrasted with gender in that sex (defined by biology at birth) is said to be natural and gender (social categories such as girl or woman that are often linked directly to sex) is said to be cultural. After all, "God created humankind in his image, in the image of God he created them; male and female he created them" (Genesis 1:27 NRSV). Sexual dimorphism (or binary sex categories) seems to simply reflect the binary pattern of creation, but sexual dimorphism and even the words *male* and *female* are cultural creations.

Though most babies are born male or female, some are born ambiguously sexed, having both male and female anatomy (due to a variety of genetic and chromosomal conditions). In the past, cultural beliefs about sexual dimorphism led doctors to surgically assign a sex to the baby, sometimes without even informing the parents. Today, parental consent is the norm, but the question of how to raise an intersex child remains ("intersex" is also called "disorders of sex development"). Should a family wait until a child is old enough to participate in decision making about surgeries, sex assignment and gender presentation? Is it better for the child if these choices are made on his or her behalf in infancy? These questions take on different dimensions depending on cultural beliefs about sex. A rigid sexual dimorphism, as Christians have often advocated based in part on the Genesis narrative, may encourage premature decision making, unwanted surgeries with unintended consequences, and shame and secrecy on the part of the intersex person and his or her family. The same belief in sexual dimorphism, held more openly, may make room for an intersex infant to grow up ambiguously sexed and even ambiguously gendered, making choices over time that are appropriate to the child's developmental stage.

Rigidly held sexual dimorphism

Openly held sexual dimorphism

Figure 1.2. Patterning the sexes

When sex is modeled as a male-female binary, intersex people are often characterized as abnormal. This approach is advocated today by some, and is not necessarily antithetical to a Christian understanding. God did create humans male and female. But sin has influenced every dimension of human life, even sexual development in utero. This is not to say that intersex people are inherently more sinful than others, only that their sex development was altered by negative genetic or chromosomal factors. Their physical abnormality is a result of our broken world. What becomes problematic is when those who don't fit the categories are dehumanized.

Imagine a different cultural world, one in which human sexual differences are not understood in binary categories, but as a spectrum. In this view, male and female still exist, but the intersex have a place on a spectrum that spans from male to female. Viewing sex as a spectrum retains the importance of sex differences for reproduction, and other distinctions between male and female, but it highlights all that we have in common as humans (male and female are positioned on the same line, not in two separate categories), and makes a more credible space for intersex persons.

Today some people take this view even further, saying that just as there is no necessary connection between biological sex and

Male ——————————— Female
Intersex

Figure 1.3. Sex as a spectrum

gender (a born male does not necessarily have to live as a man), or between gender and its social meaning (a woman does not necessarily have to express femininity with high heels or makeup), there is also no need to make sex such an important distinction between people. Social theorist Judith Butler argues that all labels, such as gender, race, ethnicity and sex, are power-laden burdens imposed on individuals. "Is there very much that follows from the fact of an originating sexual difference?" she questions.[4] Sex difference is real in her view, but it should be relatively inconsequential in society. It could be as important as eye color or earlobe size—a real difference, but not a particularly meaningful one.

I agree with Butler's emphasis on how social roles can burden people, but I believe there is, actually, very much that follows from the fact of an originating sexual difference. Being born male or female is a burden insofar as sex is a factor in social inequality around crime, violence, income, body-image issues and so on. But minimizing the difference between sexes seems to belittle the importance of human reproduction and the delight that men and women find in relationship with one another. So I think it's important to reduce sex-based inequalities, but also important to highlight the reality of being created male and female.

While human concepts and systems of understanding are probably never faultless, they can be in greater or lesser harmony with the pattern of creation. I believe that any of the three options for understanding sex—rigidly held sexual dimorphism, openly held sexual dimorphism or sex as a spectrum—could fit with a Christian understanding of creation. Each of the views has strengths and weaknesses, and each reflects the reality that God created humans male and female and charged them with being fruitful and multiplying.

Naming God's Creation

When I facilitate workshops on sexuality, I set chairs for participants in a circle and include an extra chair that remains empty. To begin the workshop, I tape a sign on the empty chair that reads, "Is homosexuality a sin?" This question is very important, but it tends to be a conversation hog, trying to turn all other dialogue into a discussion of itself. Standing in front of the chair, I say to the question, "You'll get your turn, but it's not your turn right now."

The question "Is homosexuality a sin?" presupposes that homosexuality is a thing about which valid moral judgments can be made, and it also implies that judging is the first and/or most important thing Christians need to do when they encounter homosexuality or homosexuals. This book is an effort to redirect our judging energy into critical thinking: to reflect on homosexuality, which exists hand-in-hand with heterosexuality, which links to sexuality in general, which links to humanity, which links to God, which links to holiness and discipleship and grace and love. Drop off the last two words, and you've still got an interesting question: *Is* homosexuality? And if it has *is-ness*—if it is real—what kind of real? Is it a category that accurately patterns God's creation, or one that distorts our understanding?

After God created all the animals and birds, God "brought them to the man to see what he would name them; and whatever the man called each living creature, that was its name" (Genesis 2:19). I've often pictured Adam's work as somewhat trivial; God did the hard work of making creatures, and Adam just dreamed up creative names for them. But on further reflection, I see that Adam's work was, in fact, very important. God left real work undone and waited to see what Adam would do. Adam's choices carried consequences; whatever he called the living creatures, those were their names.

When we name, label, sort and categorize, we are doing work like Adam's. The consequences of faulty naming are grave; for example, when Europeans labeled Africans "primates" instead of "humans," it legitimated slavery and all manner of cruelty. Labeling humans "male" and "female" also has consequences—for everyone, including people who are ambiguously sexed. Linking sex to gender is another complex task: what does it mean that a person is male or female? Must males live as men, and females as women? How will we name, value and treat people who live otherwise? Defining gender roles is yet another complication: if a male lives as a man, what characteristics do men have? My main interest here is sexual identity. What are the important elements of human sexuality, and how should we name them? Should sexuality be labeled and sorted at the level of human identity?

Perceiving the social construction of sexual identity categories may lead to deeper considerations about the social construction of gender roles, gender categories, sex categories and, ultimately, everything else. In my conservative Christian upbringing, I learned to equate "culture" with "the world." I saw the world as set against the church, and my goal as a Christian was to reject culture and worldliness, living only by biblical teachings. In studying cultural anthropology, I've learned that culture is like air: it's a God-given gift vital for human survival and flourishing. That culture influences every human thought and word is not a disappointment; it's an expression of our humanity.[5] As our minds are transformed, we will craft social constructs—words, phrases, concepts and systems—that help us live well in God's world.

The Trouble
with Heterosexuality

During my 1980s adolescence, my friends and I knew about various sexual identities, but heterosexuality was the only acceptable one. Our public schools didn't have gay-straight alliances or diversity workshops, fag jokes were still considered funny at school, and at church homosexuality was a superlatively bad sin about which we ought not to even speak. AIDS was poorly understood and rapidly spreading. I was advised to never touch a homosexual and heard public policy discussion about quarantining persons with AIDS on an island. It was important for me and my classmates to be perceived as heterosexual; kids worked hard to avoid or challenge accusations of gayness.

In junior high youth group, my youth pastor began "the sex talk" by handing out 3" x 5" cards and pens and then saying, "Please write any questions you have, and I'll answer them." I had recently learned about married sex from James Dobson and Elisabeth Elliot books, and I was wondering about homosexual sex. How was it done? Which parts touched which parts? If it didn't potentially produce babies, then was it really even sex? My pen was poised above my index card, but my inner voice warned, *Don't write it. If you're the only person writing, then they'll all know it was you and they'll think you're gay.* My inner voice was right: for fear of being seen writing, no one wrote any questions. Sadly, for me it was better to remain ignorant than to risk having my heterosexuality called into question.

My college students receive some of these messages, but not with the clarion call with which I heard them. On the one hand, same-sex sexualities are normalized in mass media, and public school students are taught to be accepting and tolerant of all forms of diversity, including sexual. But on the other hand, heterosexuality continues to be the privileged norm, so much so that adolescent sexual minorities experience hatred and violence. There are more sexualities to choose from, more resources for support and more encouragement to explore sexual feelings as an indicator of identity. At the same time, there are stronger warnings about the viability—even the sheer physical safety—of living out a minority sexual identity.

Students hear a cacophony of messages, and as a result, so do I. One day I talk with a student about her same-sex relationship. She's "out and proud" and is determined to change the student-life policies of her Christian college. The next day I hear from a male student who has been harassed for years for being gay. But he's not always gay. He has had same-sex encounters, but is currently with a girlfriend and wants to be married to a woman in the future. His classmates, however, some of whom he's known since high school, mock him for being "once gay, always gay." One student wants to read more about same-sex sexualities in other cultures for a class research project. Another is shocked and offended that same-sex issues are even discussed at a Christian college; she expects silence as an expression of purity.

My college students are coming of age in a world different from that of my adolescence, and seemingly on a different planet than earlier generations. My dad was a teenager in the 1950s, living in small towns across Nebraska and Iowa. I've heard his stories over and over: boy loved dog, bike and basketball. Boy grew up, met smart young woman at Baptist young adult fellowship, got married and then there was me.

I asked him, "Dad, when you were a teenager, did anyone encourage you to explore your sexual identity?" "What are you talking about?" was his reply, and the conversation moved to a more comfortable topic (dogs, probably, or basketball). Growing up to have gender, sexual desire and sexual identity all line up (in a *straight* line) was the norm, and people who fit the norm didn't need to think about it much. People who didn't fit the norm repressed their differences, expressed themselves in closeted ways, insisted on being different in unaccepting environments or moved to places (mostly large cities) where supportive networks for people of same-sex sexuality had been developing for decades.[1]

Dad's dad, a fundamentalist Baptist pastor, probably didn't think of himself as being heterosexual, and possibly didn't have a sexual identity at all. *Heterosexual* was a medical term earlier in the twentieth century, not used in everyday parlance until the 1930s.[2] We could say Grandpa was heterosexual because he fits our understanding of that word, but we'd be projecting our culture into the past. To be heterosexual requires people to believe that about themselves, in a cultural context of others who recognize "heterosexual" as a meaningful social role. Heterosexuality in that sense didn't exist in Grandpa's day; just being a man summed it up. Sexual feelings and attractions had to be managed, but his fundamentalist framework would have cast the issue in terms of sin and virtue, more like earlier centuries of Christian thought. He would not have linked sexual feelings to human identity, as we do today.

Though people did not tend to think of themselves in categories like heterosexual and homosexual, even in Grandpa's day—the early twentieth century—people with same-sex attractions and in same-sex relationships formed supportive communities in cities through shared housing, recreational centers, bars and restaurants, and other gathering places. They referred to their identities largely in terms of gender, that is, men and women, and associated themselves with movements such as free love, socialism, anarchy and feminism. Critics spoke of them with various terms: *urning, tribad, invert* or *homosexual* (a new term that wasn't widely used). But neither they nor their critics used an identity category to describe the entire group (such as sexual minority or gay-lesbian).[3]

While I appreciate Grandpa's legacy of religious devotion, his Christian message was preached to a culture very unlike mine. Theology that privileged marital sex, in Grandpa's day and earlier, takes on new meaning in today's world: it privileges heterosexual persons over all other persons. Because sexuality has moved center stage in defining human identity, heterocentrist theology constructs a hierarchy of persons. Even humble heterosexual Christians who make every effort to be kind and gracious toward homosexuals are not really reaching out; they're reaching down from a place of moral elevation. My student Michael felt alienated from his sister when she came out as a lesbian, not because of her attitude or his but because the sexual identity categories themselves created a chasm between lesbian and straight. The same is true within communities of faith. The problem isn't only that heterosexual Christians are self-righteous; it's that they're heterosexual.

The verse that follows Romans 12:1-2 is this: "For by the grace given me I say to every one of you: Do not think of yourself more highly than you ought, but rather think of yourself with sober judgment, in accordance with the faith God has distributed to each of you." Because most Christians have absorbed cultural categories of sexual identity, they see people as heterosexual or homosexual. Scriptural prohibitions against sex between people of the same sex, then, seem to denigrate the people, not just their actions. Scriptural affirmation of sex between a man and a woman in marriage seems to uplift these people, and others who want to be married, in their personhood. Instead of questioning the validity of sexual identity altogether, Christians have mostly focused on either morally elevating heterosexuality over homosexuality or equalizing all sexual identities as blessed. No matter how much Christians try to focus on behavior and not identity ("love the sinner, hate the sin"), the sexual identity framework itself draws human identity in to evaluations of human sexuality. Focusing first on heterosexuality begins to show the shortcomings of the sexual identity framework, issuing a call for the end of sexual identity.

Development of (the Thought of) Heterosexuality

Sexual identity is a Western, nineteenth-century formulation of what it means to be human. It's grounded in a belief that the direction of one's sexual desire is identity-constituting, earning each individual a label (gay, lesbian, straight, etc.) and social role. Perceived as innate and as stemming from inner desire, sexual identity has to be searched out, found, named and expressed in order for each person to be a fully functional and happy adult. Finding our sexual feelings is part of how we come to know ourselves and present ourselves to others.

Heterosexuality is a sexual identity category, and because people believe in it, it has real social and personal impact. It is also an idea that came from somewhere—it's a concept that has a history, albeit a relatively short one. Of all humans who have ever lived, very few have had sexual identities. Defined in a wide variety of ways, social identities related to sex (such as male and female) and gender (such as boy and girl) are common across world cultures. Identity categories based in sexuality (such as heterosexual and homosexual) are much less common. Most cultures that have ever been present on the earth, including biblical ones, didn't have heterosexuals. They didn't have homosexuals either, because heterosexuality requires homosexuality; each makes sense only with reference to the other. Like fraternal twins, they may not look alike, but they shared a common gestation.

Neither word existed early on in U.S. history. Sex was understood in the colonial era primarily in terms of procreation. Sexual

pleasure was important—for example, female orgasm was often
considered necessary for conception—but not essential for identity, personal happiness or self-actualization. Wayward desires or
practices were described with words like *fornication, adultery,
masturbation* or *sodomy*. It was a family-centered, reproductive
and religious sexual world; sexuality was something that existed
more *between* people in families (in one sense) and in churches (in
a different sense) than *within* an individual.[4]

In the nineteenth century, sex was still viewed as important for
procreation, and the ideal of intimacy and friendship between
spouses that is nurtured by sex became increasingly important.
Still, people did not think of themselves as having sexual identities. The labels "heterosexual" and "homosexual" emerged in the
late nineteenth century, but medical doctors were the ones using
the terms.[5] Moreover, both types of people were deviants because
they pursued sexual pleasure without concern for procreation: homosexuals with people of the same sex, heterosexuals with people
of the opposite sex (or, in some definitions, both sexes).

Well into the twentieth century, there was no word at all for
what most considered healthy and normal sexuality, that is, sex
between a man and a woman that did not involve contraception.
Gender identity ("man" or "woman") assumed proper sexuality;
only deviants were labeled. The words *heterosexual* and *homosexual* weren't used in mainstream U.S. print until around the 1930s,
and in popular understandings, proper sexuality between men and
women remained linked to procreation until the 1960s. Then, as
contraception became more accessible and reliable, sexual identities became linked almost entirely to sexual feelings, as they are
today. Reproduction, family and religion have become optional
components of sex (though vital for those who choose them), and
sexuality has taken on new meaning as an essential force that exists not between persons but within each individual, one that is
expected to provide personal identity and happiness.

The Biblical Problem with Heterosexuality

In each class I teach related to sexuality, I "come out" as no longer heterosexual. On the one hand, this is inane. I'm happily married to a man, and I'm a mother, an evangelical and a Christian college professor, all of which mark me as heterosexual. I reap the social benefits of being perceived as heterosexual in society and in Christian settings. But, as I tell students in class, I don't want to be heterosexual. I don't want to get life, secure my moral standing or gird my marriage with a social identity that privileges some and maligns others on the basis of inner desires and feelings. Heterosexuality is a concept riddled with problems. I'd even call it an abomination.

The fact that heterosexuality is a social construction isn't what's problematic. We need identity constructs in order to function; personally, I rely on notions like "professor" and "Pennsylvanian" on a daily basis. It's even possible to "Christianize" social constructs, either explicitly (making a Christian film or a starting a Christian college) or implicitly (expressing the fruits of the Spirit in any endeavor, without labeling it "Christian"). The major problem for Christians with heterosexuality, and sexual identity in general, is that it is a social construct that provides a faulty pattern for understanding what it means to be human, linking desire to identity in a way that violates biblical themes. No pattern is perfect, but this one isn't even close. And "Christianizing" sexual identity—whether by affirming or negating the morality of various sexual identities—doesn't help, because it doesn't address the faulty connections that sexual identity categories make between human desire and identity.

Heterosexuality implies that what you want, sexually speaking, is who you are. A pervasive biblical theme, however, is that human desire is fickle, a mystery even to ourselves. Eugene Peterson's paraphrase of Jeremiah 17:9-10 is helpful: "The heart is hopelessly dark and deceitful, a puzzle that no one can figure out. But I, God, search the heart and examine the mind. I get to the heart of the human. I get to the root of things. I treat them as they really are, not as they pretend to be" *(The Message)*. We are known by God more truly than we will ever know ourselves. And even when living righteously, we, like Paul, find ourselves wanting things we don't want to want and doing things we don't want to do. Desire is not a trustworthy indicator of human identity (more on this in chapter five).

Swept along with the development of the societies in which they live, however, Christians have come to believe that what a person does sexually represents more than just adherence to or violation of God's law; it determines the kind of person you are. And though many Christians continue to separate identity from behavior ("love the sinner, hate the sin"), by affiliating with heterosexuality ourselves we show our acquiescence to the notion that the sin (or the holiness) is, really, linked to the sinner (or saint). For the most part, we have laid a moral grid over preexisting cultural frameworks, and have not made new culture ourselves.

The Scientific Problem with Heterosexuality

Though they are often seen as credible because of their scientific origins, "homosexuality" and "heterosexuality" are not stable or even very accurate descriptions of human sexuality. Their definitions have shifted numerous times over the years, which means there has never been a sustained scientific consensus about what they mean. For example, within a half century of the original definitions of homosexuality and heterosexuality, sexologist Alfred Kinsey argued that human sexuality is better conceptualized as a continuum than as two or three discrete categories. In the first volume (on males) of the Kinsey Reports, he wrote, "Males do not represent two discrete populations, heterosexual and homosexual. The world is not to be divided into sheep and goats. It is a fundamental of taxonomy that nature rarely deals with discrete categories. . . . The living world is a continuum in each and every one of its aspects."[6]

Controversies surrounding Kinsey's work continue today, including discussion about some research methods that were likely unethical and harmful to participants, including children. Nonetheless, his work has enduring influence: scholars today agree that there are not two or three separate "types" of humans, sexually speaking. Instead, there are ranges of behavior, fluidity in sexual feelings and complicated personal sexual histories (more on sexual fluidity in chapter five). The Kinsey Scale illustrates the possibilities, ranging from zero (exclusive heterosexuality) to six (exclusive homosexuality), with one more category for asexuality.[7]

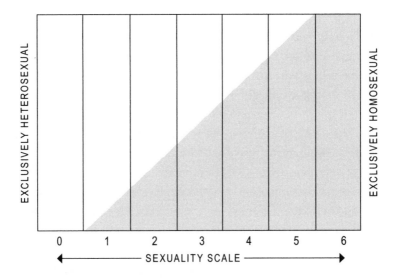

0- Exclusively heterosexual with no homosexual
1- Predominantly heterosexual, only incidentally homosexual
2- Predominantly heterosexual, but more than incidentally homosexual
3- Equally heterosexual and homosexual
4- Predominantly homosexual, but more than incidentally heterosexual
5- Predominantly homosexual, only incidentally heterosexual
6- Exclusively homosexual

Figure 2.1. Kinsey Scale (heterosexual-homosexual rating scale)

Kinsey was mostly concerned with behavior, and less with thoughts, feelings or attractions. The Klein Sexual Orientation Grid is a revision of the Kinsey Scale that measures a person's past, present and ideal responses about multiple elements of sexuality, not just behavior.[8] A person fills out each box in the grid according to the numeric options given, and then a professional assesses the numbers (some online sites do this automatically). Each person is categorized using a seven-point scale: heterosexual only, heterosexual mostly, heterosexual somewhat more, heterosexual/gay-lesbian equally, gay-lesbian somewhat more, gay-lesbian mostly or gay-lesbian only.

This grid conceptualizes Klein's primary interest, bisexuality, but also helps illuminate the complexity of human sexuality by including sexual attraction; behavior; thoughts and fantasies; emotional bonding; patterns of socializing; lifestyle issues like shopping or vacationing or neighborhood preference; and self-identification—at the present, in the past and as one hopes to be in the future. Most people in our society report consistent opposite-sex sexuality (women inclined toward men and men toward women) across these measures. But those who are non-heterosexual in some way(s) are more numerous than the small percentage of the population who self-identify as gay or lesbian. After reviewing the literature and conducting his own research, psychologist Roy Baumeister concludes that "erotic plasticity" (what others, including me, call "sexual fluidity") is more than just youthful experimentation or confusion.[9] Many humans have capacity for sexual feelings toward both sexes, though women report greater fluidity than men.

In Edward Laumann's research (discussed in chapter three), though only 1.3 percent of women described themselves as homosexual or bisexual, over 8 percent of women had some adult same-sex sexuality (could be desire or behavior). For men, though only 2.4 percent defined themselves as homosexual or bisexual, 10 percent had some adult same-sex sexuality.[10] In another study, also on

	Past (entire life up until a year ago)	Present (last 12 months)	Ideal (what would you like?)
A – Sexual Attraction: To whom are you sexually attracted?			
B – Sexual Behaviour: With whom have you actually had sex?			
C – Sexual Fantasies: About whom are your sexual fantasies			
D - Emotional preference: Who do you feel more drawn to or close to emotionally?			
E - Social preference: Which gender do you socialize with?			
F - Lifestyle preference: In which community do you like to spend your time? In which do you feel most comfortable?			
G - Self-identification: How do you label or identify yourself?			

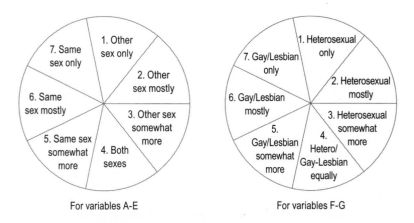

For variables A-E   For variables F-G

Figure 2.2. Klein Sexual Orientation Grid. Using the pieces of the pie chart, fill in your answers to the above questions.

a national scale, sociologist Mark Regnerus reports that, among fifteen- to nineteen-year-olds, 5.4 percent of boys and 15.5 percent of girls are at least sometimes attracted to members of the same sex, though less than 3 percent of boys and around 7 percent of girls self-identify as homosexual or bisexual.[11]

The scientific problem with heterosexuality is that it is an imprecise category that is difficult to define or measure. It falls short as a concept for interpreting or describing human sexuality.

The Practical Problem with Heterosexuality

On a very basic level, heterosexuality is problematic because it encourages inauthenticity and even duplicity for Christians. For example, homosexuals are often seen as having particular ways of dressing and speaking, but heterosexuals do as well. Heterosexual men wear very limited colors and fabrics, choose from only a few hairstyles, use relatively more space in their walk and stance, and display a limited range of facial expressions and emotion. When new fashion trends emerge, like earrings, the color pink or bags, heterosexual men have to determine whether these will mark them as fashionable-straight or flaming-gay. Traits as innocuous as not wearing ruffles and lace, or as significant as restraining emotional tenderness or showcasing violence, are social markers of masculinity and heterosexuality.

Despite growing acceptance of sexual diversity among some, many boys learn at a young age to perform heterosexuality properly or pay a steep price. In a class discussion about gender socialization, Jeremy described how frustrated he gets when his seven-year-old brother Tre cries about falling down or making a mistake in a game. Jeremy recounted, "I say to him, 'Grow up, man! Quit acting like a girl!'"

I questioned, "Why is crying girlish, and why do you call a little boy 'man'?"

Jeremy laughed, "It's not like I'm in a gender studies class all the time! I don't want my little brother to be teased for being girly. And besides, I get tired of listening to him cry."

The power of socially defined gender and sex roles comes from the fact that they aren't clearly spelled out in a document or law. People teach and reinforce them to each other through relationships in families, churches, schools and society at large. In this example, sexual identity and gender roles go hand in hand; being seen as "girly" likely calls into question both masculinity and heterosexuality. Tre is learning from his older brother how emotional expression is associated with manhood, and that failing to meet the norm brings derision.

I suggested that Jeremy could encourage Tre not to cry so much, but for the most straightforward reason: it grates on Jeremy's ears. Jeremy acknowledged, though, that irritation is the lesser part of the problem. Wanting his little brother to be "normal," he admitted his worry about the alternatives: "If Tre keeps crying over little things and I don't teach him to stop, then he'll be made fun of by other kids and possibly get a reputation at school that he can't shake."

Girls face these pressures too, but with more leeway. To an extent, girls can adopt boys' styles of dress, activities and patterns of speech and still be seen as feminine. Even when girls engage in same-sex intimacy, it may be more easily seen as trivial or as a phase or, stranger yet, as attractive to men. In contrast, rejecting all things feminine is a key part of heterosexual masculinity.[12]

I wondered aloud whether Jeremy might model healthy emotion for his brother, maybe even making their brotherly relationship an emotional haven for the younger boy. If swallowing tears and bolstering bravado must be part of male adolescence, Jeremy could make their home a respite instead of a reinforcer. He seemed unpersuaded. Perhaps he will follow another time-honored tradition of teaching children social lessons—even tough ones—at home first, so they are spared the embarrassment of learning them in public.

Whether it's between siblings in a family or believers in a church or other gatherings of Christians, tension exists between the gospel message of authenticity, humility and honest revelation of self in community, and the cultural reality of heterosexuality as a club with strict membership requirements. The cultural reality limits people's ability to be real with each other and creates huge barriers to addressing issues related to same-sex desire or practice. When it comes to talking about sex at church, honesty can carry dire consequences. A person may be shamed, silenced, gossiped about, harassed or harmed, and his or her basic human identity may be changed in the eyes of others. Thus, the problem with heterosexuality, for Christians, is that it sabotages our intentions to know and be known by others.

Betraying Heterosexuality

Sexual journeys are profoundly personal and private, and for many they lead down detours, into clearings, onto mountaintops and into shadows. Sexual feelings, dreams, fantasies and behaviors can be surprising or distressing. Pursuing holiness in sexuality is difficult enough, but heterosexuals are additionally hindered by cultural and religious privilege that prevents them from telling their stories honestly. I once blogged, "What if some homosexuals are in desperate pain, and our Christian affirmation of homosexuality ignores their cries?" A commenter replied, "What if some straight people are in desperate pain, and our Christian affirmation of heterosexuality ignores their cries?" Dividing people into stratified sexual groups means the privileged have to work to maintain privilege, and the subordinate are, well, subordinate. This undermines the very heart of what, as believers, we're supposed to be doing: loving each other with abandon.

Betraying heterosexuality is an important step toward restoring Christian love. English scholar Crystal Downing explains, "Embedded in the very word 'tradition' is the possibility of betrayal."[13]

Its Latin root means "to hand over," part of words such as *traitor* and *betray*. People hand over symbols, meanings and practices from generation to generation through culture. Deliberately betraying a tradition, or altering it wisely, can be just as faithful as maintaining it. Betraying heterosexuality, then, means learning to use sexual identity categories strategically (which sometimes means not using them at all), instead of being (ab)used by them when they tell us who we are, what we're worth and with whom we should associate. It's not about ignoring or isolating ourselves from society, since it is essential to understand what people mean by "gay" or "queer" or "bisexual" or whatever label, and engage in respectful dialogue. And it is sometimes important to be heterosexual, especially if using that label helps us serve others or pursue justice. Rather, betraying heterosexuality is about understanding cultural categories but not living by their power.

Sexuality, including both the good and the bad, is better understood in light of our beloved created nature, not in light of sexual desire. Identity comes from God, not sexual feelings. Take the grade point average (GPA) as an example. For most of my education, I longed for a cumulative 4.0. For years I ruminated over the D I earned in seventh-grade volleyball. That single stain on my otherwise clean academic record held me back from a 4.0. In high school, Algebra II did me in; my 3.98 felt like a failure. In my first semester of college, an A- in Introduction to Psychology ruined my goal of perfection. From junior high through college, my GPA used me. I accepted its messages about my intellect, my work ethic and even my self-worth. It hounded me, and I couldn't find a space in my life free of its judgment.

As I was applying to graduate schools, I had a thought that felt like such a betrayal that I had to whisper it to myself: *my GPA doesn't matter so much!* I realized its instrumental value: it could earn me graduate-school admission and could help pay for my education with merit-based scholarships and fellowships. But beyond that, it was no longer useful. I found freedom to learn in peace without the GPA monkey on my back. This newfound freedom was put to the test when I earned an A- in a graduate course. Just like junior high, high school and college, my graduate GPA wouldn't be a 4.0. I felt disappointed for a day or two, and then genuinely let it go. I learned to use the GPA for applications and scholarships, and to refuse to let it use me. In betraying it, I did not diminish tradition; it actually reinvigorated my experience of the academic tradition. My GPA should be interpreted in light of my lifelong love of learning, instead of what has so long been the case: my lifelong love of learning interpreted (demeaningly) by my GPA.

Who Do You Say I Am?

Twenty-first-century believers are well positioned to carry forward the tradition of Christian sexual ethics by strategically betraying sexual identity. After all, Jesus disturbed people's understanding of normal sexuality in his day; he was born to a woman who became pregnant without having sex, and he never married or had children. Believers from then until now struggle to understand Jesus' conception, birth, life and death, because each upsets taken-for-granted understandings of what it means to be human. The Christian religion is grounded in cultural disturbance, a rattling of what people take for granted.

Jesus asked his disciples at one point, "Who do people say the Son of Man is?" They replied easily, "Some say John the Baptist; others say Elijah; and still others, Jeremiah or one of the prophets" (Matthew 16:13-14 NIV). Of all the names Jesus was called (charlatan, fool and so on), the disciples parroted the most favorable misimpression of Jesus, that he was one of the prophets. Jesus didn't ask this question just because he wanted to know what people were saying about him. He was asking his disciples to rehearse their cultural categories, to turn their eyes around and look inside their own minds.

After asking the disciples to recite the common cultural interpretation of a religious prophet like himself, Jesus pushed them with a second question: "'But what about you?' he asked. 'Who do you say I am?'" Peter got it right: "You are the Messiah, the Son of the living God" (Matthew 16:15-16 NIV). Jesus praised Peter for being open to divine revelation that pushed ordinary interpretations to their rightfully divine extreme. Jesus was both culturally predictable (a Jewish teacher) and unpredictable (the Messiah). "Messiah," or "Christ," was a predictable category that helped people understand Jesus from within their tradition, but then Jesus filled that category with new meaning: the Messiah will be a suffering servant, not a nationalistic leader.[14]

In asking, "Who do people say I am?" Jesus guided his disciples in a way similar to how anthropologists teach their students, encouraging them to perceive the patterns of their world. In his second question, "Who do you say I am?" he taught discernment. This helped them be transformed by the renewing of their minds to see, speak and live a new reality, Christ's kingdom come.

Who Do We Say We Are?

We can use Jesus' approach to ask a different question: "Who do people say we are?" With respect to sexuality, people say we are heterosexual or homosexual (or straight, gay, lesbian, bisexual, queer or some other designator). People say we have sexual identities and that it's important to affiliate with one.

Believers today can do as Jesus did—use cultural categories strategically, filling the useful ones with better meaning. For some, this may mean rejecting the label of heterosexuality altogether and becoming "unlabeled" in their sexuality, which is my choice. I use my roles of being a woman (a gender category linked to biological sex) and a married person (a religious vow and life station) to define my sexuality, not the concept of *heterosexuality*. Others may wish to use heterosexuality instead of being used by it.

In a conversation with Tom, a man at my church, I encouraged him to stop putting his identity at the mercy of the homosexual-heterosexual binary. He experienced wide-ranging sexual desires and was complaining to me, "It's not that I'm gay, because I'm not. But I'm having sex with men, so I can't be straight, right? Why can't I just be Tom?"

I replied, "You can. Just be Tom, seeking counsel from other Christians as you pursue holiness in the way of Jesus." The chasm between heterosexual and homosexual may be impassable, but the space between one Christian and another can be bridged.

The Trouble
with Homosexuality

Malinda is single now, but has been in intimate relationships only with women for about ten years. Before that, she dated men and once had a male fiancé. In public she says she's thoroughly a lesbian, but in private she says she really wants to be married to someone she deeply loves, and that someone could be a man or a woman.

Jim is the father of one of my friends. Jim and his wife were both virgins when they married young, and they worked together as pastor and Sunday school coordinator for many years. When my friend left home for college, Jim left his wife to live openly as a gay man. Turns out he had been seeing male prostitutes, having male boyfriends and viewing gay pornography throughout their marriage. He says he's always been gay and regrets having used Christianity and marriage to avoid facing his true self.

Neil is a young Christian man who leads an ex-gay support group. He has never had sex with anyone, male or female, but has strong feelings of attraction toward other men and confusing sexual feelings toward women that alternate between frequent revulsion and occasional attraction. He wonders what romantic relationships might be like, and whether he might be able to be married to a woman someday. He defines himself as "ex-gay"; that's the label used in his ministry group that is his primary community.

While walking through my Washington, D.C., neighborhood, I

met a man who dressed and acted as a woman. At least, I think Joan was a male dressed as a female, but s/he could have also used female hormones to alter male physiology, or maybe even had a sex change. Or maybe she was born female. She told me a compelling story that concluded with a plea for money, which I gave, but then the very next day I overheard Joan on the Metro telling the same story to someone else. I asked around and learned that Joan was well known in the neighborhood as a homeless addict, begging, stealing and turning tricks for drugs.

Malinda, Jim, Neil and Joan could all be labeled "homosexual," but that would reveal more about the inadequacy of the term than much of anything about their lives. "Homosexuality" is a sexual identity that links sexual desire to sexual identity; who you want sexually is who you are socially. We are enculturated to think of sexual desire in this way: that it is identity-constituting, and that people who experience persistent same-sex attraction are a distinct category of persons in society. But people labeled "homosexual" are very different from one another. There are many other examples than the ones I've given, to be sure, but just these four individuals have numerous differences: male or female, married or not, sexually active or not, at peace with the sex into which they were born or not, exclusively same-sex attracted or not.

Identifying homosexuals with statistical measures is no easier. Scientists Edward Laumann, John Gagnon, Robert Michael and Stuart Michaels conducted a national survey of sexual behavior called the National Health and Social Life Study. They knew their statistic on the prevalence of homosexuality would be one of the most sought-after findings, yet they began their discussion of homosexuality with a grumble: "To quantify or count something requires unambiguous definition of the phenomenon in question. And we lack this in speaking of homosexuality."[1] They counted people's same-sex behaviors, desire, self-definition, identification and combinations of all those things over time.

They reported two Venn diagrams describing for men and for women the permutations of same-sex desire, behavior and identity. Only a small percentage of people with any same-sex sexuality were placed at the nexus of all three circles; many people experienced one or two same-sex factors, such as desire without identity or behavior, or behavior without desire. The groups at the nexus of the circles—who define themselves as homosexual or bisexual, have same-sex partners and have same-sex desire—were about 2.4 percent of all men and 1.3 percent of all women.[2] None of the people I described, however, would be counted by this statistic.

Like heterosexuality, homosexuality is an idea that has a history. It may be quickly becoming history insofar as *homosexual* has been replaced by more specific terms such as *lesbian, gay* and *bisexual*. Newer categories, however, retain the premise that sexual feelings warrant a corresponding social identity. In this sense, all sexual identity categories have a common trouble: they tell us that what a person wants, sexually, is an important measure of who a person is.

Development of (the Thought of) Homosexuality

Homosexuality is a particular pattern of same-sex relations that developed in the modern West. In many (perhaps most) societies ever present in the world there was same-sex activity but no homosexuals. Within official Western Christian frameworks, for example, same-sex acts were said to be performed by sodomites, not homosexuals, and same-sex acts were thought of in terms of morality and sin, not biology, family dynamics, psychology or other modern paradigms. The formal response to sodomy was as thoroughly religious as the understanding itself. People were called to repent, to acknowledge their sin and turn toward morality. Men and women who engaged in same-sex sex were still just men and women in their permanent social identities. Sodomite was a label that could be shed along with the sin.[3]

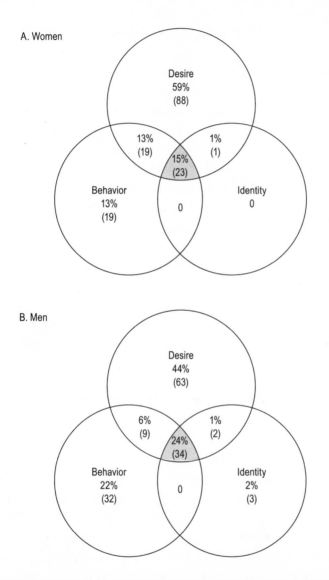

Figure 3.1. Interrelation of components of homosexuality. Diagram A describes 150 women (8.6 percent of the total sample) who reported any adult same-sex sexuality. Diagram B describes 143 men (10.1 percent of the total sample) who reported any adult same-sex sexuality. The nexus of the diagram, where a person reports all three components of same-sex sexuality (desire, behavior and identity) represents 2.4 percent of all men and 1.3 percent of all women in the study (see p. 57).

Western understandings of same-sex relations eventually shifted from the religious sphere to the legal realm, where same-sex sex became a crime and practitioners became not sinners but criminals (or, often, both sinner and criminal). Vestiges of these once-pervasive concepts remain today in Christian theology and in anti-sodomy laws, but the dominant discourse for making sense of same-sex sex shifted in the nineteenth century to the medical sphere. Beginning just over a hundred years ago, homosexuality was understood by scientists in new ways, as a degenerative disease, a form of insanity, a congenital condition or an acquired condition. Thus, a new type of human being emerged: the homosexual.

Today, same-sex sexuality is studied in a variety of disciplines, including biology, sociology, anthropology and psychology, and people of same-sex attraction are less often labeled "homosexual" as though they constitute a subspecies of humans. Though many Christians continue to use the term *homosexual,* the word is often rejected today, in part because it groups too many different kinds of people together in a single category, illustrated by the examples of Jim, Malinda, Joan and Neil. Sexual identity categories have proliferated (gay, lesbian, bisexual and so on), but they share with "homosexuality" the assumption that the orientation of a person's sexuality constitutes identity.

Like jeans and music, the Western concept of sexual identity is being exported around the world. People in other societies, with other notions of sexuality and identity, are adopting Western "homosexuality," shaping their self-presentation and even self-identities accordingly. For instance, Garret Keizer describes how Ugandans have known of same-sex intimacy, particularly between adolescent friends, but have considered it a temporary and relatively innocuous part of childhood sexual exploration. Drawn into Western frameworks via the Anglican church conflict over homosexuality, Ugandans have now been introduced to—and some are choosing to absorb—Western concepts that make same-sex attraction mean something more than it has earlier.[4] Even in a culture as remote as the Bugis, people are beginning to identify as lesbian instead of *calalai,* and as gay or transgender instead of *calabai,* because Western identities carry more cachet.

The reality is that same-sex feelings and behaviors take on different configurations and meanings in various cultures, and they change over time. Thus, the notion that people have sexual identities is a social construct: because people believe it, it becomes real in its effects.

The Origins of Homosexuality

Today, most people believe sexual identity is located within the individual. When a person asks, "Why are people gay?" the answer often puts the individual at the center of the frame and offers evidence from genetics or psychology. Though those fields of study are different than my own—which focuses on how people learn to embody cultural meanings, beliefs and behaviors—the biological, genetic and psychological origins of same-sex desire are intriguing to me too.

The bottom line is that scientists don't yet understand all the factors that shape sexual desire.[5] Current research focuses on genetics, the prenatal hormonal environment, family (birth order, twin and adoption studies), and biological research on nonsexual physical traits such as right- or left-handedness, finger length, height, weight, inner-ear characteristics, and body morphology. (The idea is that perhaps non-normative biology in nonsexual parts of the body relates to sexual development.) As researchers replicate earlier studies, they sometimes get conflicting results and, most interesting to me, disagree about what exactly it is they're studying. Depending on preferred theory and methods, scientists measure different variables as indicative of sexual identity, including sexual desire, thoughts, feelings, behaviors, intimate relationships, self-identification, fantasy or achievement of orgasm.

When people ask about the origins of homosexuality, they aren't usually asking for an anthropology lesson, but I believe the anthropological contribution is essential. Desires, however biologically grounded, are formed by culture; we can't want what we don't know. For example, though I share with most humans a concern for personal appearance, I have never longed to extend my neck with stacks of neck bracelets, as some Southeast Asian and African women do, or to create beautiful patterns of scarring on my face, as a Nuer woman in East Africa might. These technologies and beliefs about beauty aren't taught or recognized in my society. I do, however, believe that painting dark lines across my lower eyelids and brushing pink powder on my cheeks makes my face more beautiful. Anthropologist Pat Caplan summarizes, "What people want, and what they do, in any society, is to a large extent what they are made to want, and allowed to do. Sexuality . . . cannot escape its cultural connection."[6]

In terms of sexual ethics, it is all too easy for some Christians to claim that homosexuality stems from "nurture," and therefore that all homosexuals need to do is choose to change. This is a vestige of premodern Christian thought, when same-sex activity was thought of purely in terms of behavior and in religious terms: the sodomite needs to repent. That line of reasoning simply doesn't fit the world today. Even scientists who emphasize "nurture" agree that homosexuality is not always freely chosen, or that it's not always possible to change orientation. Try changing your language, food taboos, definition of beauty, smell preferences or sense of personal space. These are all nongenetic, learned traits, but they are very resistant to change.

Other Christians affirm homosexuality by appealing to "nature." If people are created gay, the argument goes, then how can a person be condemned for simply being as God made her or him? Like the opposing argument, this line of reasoning selects only the science that fits a specific theological point of view. And it fails to recognize that scientists in biology, genetics or psychology who emphasize "nature" acknowledge social factors that influence the development of the trait they study. Even traits that seem overwhelmingly genetic or biological, like intelligence or athletic ability, are shaped by the social and physical environment, even prenatally.

Theology, ethics and ways of reading Scripture can't rely on an airtight understanding of the origins of same-sex sexuality. Instead, Christian dialogue should be responsive to both the knowing and the not-knowing of contemporary science. We should be fair about appropriating scientific research into Christian thought, resisting the temptation to pick and choose science that seems to support a preexisting point of view.

Same-Sex Sexuality: The Patterns of the World

It may seem odd to speak of same-sex sex being patterned or organized, especially to Christians who view homosexual acts as separate from homosexual persons. The "hate the sin, love the sinner" approach treats sexual behaviors like other behaviors—for example, bicycling or basket-weaving—that a person can fairly easily choose to stop. But whether it's with a spouse or someone else, and whether it's with someone of the same sex or opposite, sex is often more than just a behavior. It may not always be linked to identity or personhood, but it's always linked to some set of meanings, values and relationships. Behavior is never isolated from context. For instance, take something even simpler than sex, say bicycling. Bicycling is linked to cultural values like health and relationships; at times it can also be linked to social status, recreational communities and even profession. Those who really love it might even say bicycling is linked to the soul, which makes sense for sex too.

Scholars in recent years, many of whom are either LGBTQ (lesbian-gay-bisexual-transgender-queer) themselves or advocates for LGBTQ concerns, have hoped that anthropologists could make the case that homosexuality exists in many cultures. They reason that if homosexuality is proven to be common, not rare, it would support the view that it should not be stigmatized. As they considered the data, however, many shifted to a new perspective: while same-sex sex occurs in many cultures, homosexuality (a social label and role based on a same-sex-oriented sexual identity) is rare. Sociologist Stephen Murray cataloged hundreds of descriptions of same-sex sexual behavior from ethnographies, anthropologists' written descriptions of other ways of life.[7] He argues that across world cultures, there are many instances of same-sex sex, but there are only a few ways these relationships are socially patterned: age-structured, gender-structured, profession-based and egalitarian (more about each of these below). When it comes to same-sex sex, this is the "pattern of the world."

A side note of reassurance: if this material is challenging for you, it is also for me. A Christian friend (from a similarly sheltered background as mine) was sitting next to me in graduate school when we started learning about sexuality in crosscultural perspective. During a lecture on public gay sex, she whispered to me, "Their glory is in their shame" (Philippians 3:19). As for me, I memorized psalms and jotted them in the margins of my notes as a way of spiritually protecting myself from the challenging information I heard on a regular basis. In retrospect, I think my friend and I were doing the best we could. We came from Christian backgrounds that encouraged what we might call mental hygiene; holiness required personal cleanness, keeping your distance from defiling things, even information about defiling things. We used the Bible like antibacterial soap to keep us clean. I've come to see the Bible and my faith in a different light—as salt instead of soap. Instead of standing aside washing my hands, I engage anything and everything in God's world for the purpose of being a blessing.

Others may find the material challenging because it seems to diminish the prevalence, or even the existence, of LGBTQ people (if "homosexuality" is just a social construct, then maybe homosexual people are too). Murray and others make a strong case that it simply isn't accurate to label those of same-sex attraction in other societies "homosexual." Today, anthropologists document same-sex sexuality and find that it is fairly prevalent around the world. Instead of trying to make the case that same-sex sexuality elsewhere is just like ours, it is more fruitful to describe the many different ways that people link together sex, gender and sexuality, and the many different ways that societies and religions interpret human sexuality.

Age-structured same-sex relationships. Found around the world, age-structured same-sex relationships are pairings in which an age difference between partners is essential. In ancient Greece, for instance, men sometimes took boy lovers. Ideally, the adult would experience sexual passion but the boy wouldn't; the boy should be learning about love and friendship in their purest form. The boy wasn't feminized and didn't become gay; he just provided a temporary sexual outlet for a man. Greeks understood ideal friendship as flourishing between equals, and men and women were never equal. In fact, if a man showed too much love for a woman, his manhood could be called into question. If he showed occasional sexual interest in boys, however, this likely proved the strength of his sexual appetite and manhood.[8]

As is the case for every category of same-sex relationships, much less evidence exists about women. This may be because fewer women than men have same-sex relationships or, more likely, because women's experiences and perspectives were recorded less often.[9] Some fragments of literature and images on vases from Sparta and Lesbos suggest a woman-girl teaching relationship in which women prepared girls for marriage, but it is hard to say whether girls were just told about sex or were initiated into it.

When Paul wrote about *malakos* and *arsenokoites* (1 Corinthians 6:9 and 1 Timothy 1:10—two passages commonly cited in condemnation of homosexuality), it was likely in reference to age-structured same-sex relations. In the Roman world, sex was linked to masculinity, but not in the way we would make the connection. It was more something a man did *to* someone else—a way of expressing power and privilege—and less something shared *with* a lover; the status of the persons involved was more important than the gender or the type of sex. The Romans saw the insertive role as masculine and the receptor role as feminine, so if a man had the insertive role in a sexual encounter with a male or female of lower status, then he was acting as a male. A free man, then, could have sex with a slave (boy or girl) or a boy prostitute, but should not have sex with freeborn girls or boys. (Note that the very phrase "have sex with" reveals *our* cultural bias.) In light of this, a man enjoying a loving, committed relationship with a male of equal status may have been laughable; for free men, at least, sex was more about pleasure and power, and less about friendship, commitment or love. Romans also assimilated Greek beliefs about male friendship and warriorhood, believing that sex with boys masculinized the youth.[10]

The question of Paul's cultural knowledge of same-sex relations is inherently a difficult one. Historical evidence is limited, and the Roman Empire covered a lot of ground, so it's hard to make valid generalizations about the entire Roman Empire, including Paul's various locations. Scholars have recorded exceptions to and broader interpretations of these generalizations about Roman same-sex sexuality. In addition, there is literary evidence of loving, long-term same-sex relationships between men, and of relations between high-status Roman men and freeborn boys and girls. Some argue that Roman sexual ideals around the time of Christ are best viewed as numerous, including a high value on procreative, marital sex with room for same-sex relations among youth, between dominant men and social subordinates, and between men as equals.[11]

For our purposes, the point is that age-structured same-sex relationships are not the same as homosexuality; these relationships
would be illegal and unethical in our society. They also don't meet
the ideals of equality, friendship, intimacy and partnership associated with today's same-sex relationships.

   Gender-structured same-sex relationships. Gender-structured same-sex relationships hinge on the different gender roles of
the partners; how gender works in the relationship is more important than the sexual feelings and practices of the partners. One
example, found with variations across South America, the Caribbean, Mesoamerica and the Mediterranean, is the *activo-pasivo*
pairing, a traditional relational form that continues to exist alongside more modern egalitarian same-sex relations. An *activo* is a
hypermasculine man who desires only penetrative sex, preferably
with women but sometimes also with *pasivos*, men willing to be
penetrated. Too much same-sex indulgence or emotional attach-
ment calls the *activo's* masculinity into question, but not just the
act of same-sex sex or the desire for it. Often, the *pasivo* acts feminine and is assumed to have traits generally associated with women,
like being emotional, being sexually responsive and needing provi-
sion (they often accept money for sex, but are not seen as prostitutes). They "play up" their femininity, but unlike proper women,
they are unabashed and boastful about their sexuality. The *pasivo,*
then, is seen as having compromised his masculinity, while the
activo remains a typical male. Thus, though sexuality is obviously
important in this case, gender performance defines social roles,
not sexual desire or behavior.[12]

   Another example of gender-structured same-sex relationships
comes from Samoa, where a man who dresses as a woman and
flaunts his sexuality and beauty is *fa'afafine*, which means "like a
woman." *Fa'afafine* often have sex with men, but their role is more
gender-defined, based on the desire of a man to look and act like a
woman. Sexual desire and practice are therefore not the most im-

portant elements in their identity, making their same-sex relationships distinct from the Western concept of homosexuality.[13]

Gender-based same-sex relations are present in our society to some extent. The butch-femme pairing of women in the mid-twentieth century comes closest to gender-based relations.[14] Butches dressed and acted as masculine as possible, even emulating male violence. The femme was a more feminine lesbian whose relationship with the butch mirrored male-female heterosexual relationships in society. Less is known about sexual relations between butches and femmes; in any case, performing their gender roles was at least as important as sexual feelings and expression. The butch-femme lesbian ideal has faded over the last fifty years, but it still shapes American stereotypes of homosexuality. When people ask of lesbian (and gay) couples, "Who's the man and who's the woman?" they inaccurately presume that same-sex relationships always imitate mainstream gender norms.

Profession-based same-sex relationships. Entertainer, prostitute and religious specialist are the three most common professions for people whose work necessitates sexual nonconformity. (An interesting trio of professions! I'd love to listen in on a conversation between members of any of these groups discussing what they might have in common with the others.) One example, documented in over a hundred Native American tribes, is the two-spirit (formerly *berdache*). Most of the documentation we have comes from European anthropologists and colonizers, so we know little about Native peoples' own historical understandings of two-spirits, including their sexual practices.[15] However, we do know that a two-spirit is a man or woman who dresses like and does the work of the other gender. The person may also perform spiritual rituals around childbirth, marriage and death.

The Bugis making room for spiritually gifted intersex children to become priests is another example. Similarly, some ethnic groups in Siberia, Borneo and the Philippines have designated religious roles for people of ambiguous sexual biology or those of same-sex attraction. It is sometimes unclear whether the persons involved are inherently same-sex attracted or gender-bending, or if they perform these roles as a way of making a living.[16] This is clearly different, then, than the Western notion of homosexuality as a "real" quality residing within the individual and modern beliefs about the importance of harmonizing sexual practice with sexual feelings.

Egalitarian same-sex relationships. Egalitarian same-sex relationships are the cultural ideal for same-sex relations in many contemporary societies, including the United States. In these relationships, partners are of approximately equal social status and age and the relationship is marked by reciprocity and mutuality. Found in various world cultures, these types of relationships are usually short-term and take place before or alongside heterosexual marriage.[17] It is less common for an egalitarian same-sex relationship to replace male-female marriage, as in Western societies today.

Ancient Greek and Roman artifacts and literature show long-term, loving, same-sex sexual relationships between social equals. Early in the twentieth century, anthropologist Melville Herskovits described same-sex intimacies between friends as a normal part of adolescence in Dahomey (now Benin). Anthropologists today, however, debate about whether contemporary egalitarian relations in other societies are indigenous or influenced by Western traditions.

The modern "homosexual" is a new configuration of sexuality in which those of same-sex attraction comprise a distinct group within which exists the possibility of relationships that are egalitarian and exclusive, possibly lifelong. Long-term same-sex relationships existed before the twentieth century, even when social norms may have required lovers to remain single or in heterosexual marriages. Though the interpersonal dynamic may be similar, these examples would not be categorized as "homosexual" because people in such relationships were not recognized as a distinct social group. Homosexuality does not require gender non-conformity; a gay person may remain fully the gender he or she was at birth and may dress and act the same as heterosexuals of the same gender. Gender nonconformity used to be a more significant part of American homosexuality (gay men being feminine and lesbians being masculine), but this has diminished greatly in the last half century.

The pattern of same-sex relations in modern Western societies is only one among the various patterns of same-sex sex in the world. Same-sex sex takes on meaning within culture, which links sex, gender, desire, behavior and identity in particular ways. These meanings change over time, partly with a society's internal changes and partly from contact with other societies.

Sexual Others

Homosexual is too specific a term to describe the same-sex practices of the ancient Greeks, Samoans, Latin Americans, Native Americans, Bugis and the myriad other societies that have ever been present on the earth. It's too narrow to even describe Malinda, Jim, Neil and Joan, and they're all living in the same society. None of them meet the definition of the modern homosexual, a person of exclusive same-sex attraction in an egalitarian same-sex relationship. Malinda's attractions include both men and women. Jim had (and still has) great love for his wife, and had enough attraction to her to at least have procreative sex. For over twenty years his homosexuality was more about fantasy, pornography, sexual encounters with relative strangers and paying for sex. None of these sexual expressions included friendship, mutual support or commitment. I never learned anything about Joan's sexuality—not even whether she is male or female. In fact, if she is a cross-dressing man attracted to women, then she isn't homosexual at all. And Neil has no sexual experience but identifies very strongly with a homosexual identity, in part because it provides entrée into the "ex-gay" world of Christian support and community.

The concept "homosexual" really functions as a category of negation, containing all who are not heterosexual. The label tells us virtually nothing about an individual other than the single fact that she or he is not heterosexual. It just doesn't make sense to lump diverse individuals together as "homosexuals" and then claim the Bible has a single message of condemnation that covers each of their situations; doing so reduces the complexity of a human life to a single abominable term. By condemning homosexuality with such vehemence, Christians have arguably contributed to the cementing of sexual desire as central to human identity. Sociologist Jeffrey Weeks, a scholar of the emergence of homosexuality and heterosexuality as social categories in the modern Western world, concludes, "Women and men have mobilized around their sense of sexual identity . . . because it was in their sexuality that they felt most powerfully invalidated."[18]

I saw this happen to Michelle, a friend at church who was in a same-sex relationship. She didn't think her same-sex relationship was pleasing to God, but at the same time she found great love and companionship with her partner. She was genuinely torn. At church, it seemed that people were overly concerned with persuading Michelle to end her relationship and stop being a lesbian. A pastor even said that while she was welcome to bring her partner to church, they should not hold hands or otherwise reveal their relationship to anyone. In the lesbian community of her town, however, people were warm and accepting, even of the fact that Michelle attended a non-gay-affirming church. She said to me, "It seems like I have to choose between my sexuality and my spirituality." Eventually, partly because her spiritual community kept honing in on her sin rather than caring about her life as a whole, she did leave the church, and later left Christianity altogether.

My colleague Mindy Michels, an anthropologist and also a lesbian involved in activism around LGBTQ issues, complained to me that Christians often use military metaphors to discuss LG-BTQ issues. I readily acknowledged her point; my entire life I've heard Christians talk about homosexuals as our opponents in the "culture wars" and stress the importance of "fighting," "mobilizing" and "defeating" the "enemy." I pushed back at Mindy's comment, however, wondering whether LGBTQ activist discourse does the same thing. We researched the issue and coauthored an article about how LGBTQ activists and conservative Christians share a commitment to violent language, citing gay and lesbian activists who talk about "strategies and tactics" for "fighting the Right," and Christians who say homosexuals are "evil" and that the church should become "militant" and "aggressive" for righteousness.[19] Our conclusion was that, despite the deep differences between gay and lesbian activists and conservative Christians, they might agree that violence is wrong and change their approach in light of the abundant evidence that violent speech promotes physical violence.

Processes of "othering" should alert us to probable injustice. Groups of people create "us" and "them" categories for self-protection, designating a subgroup of humanity (often based on nationality, religion, race, language and other similar characteristics) to whom one owes loyalty and resource-sharing. It follows that "they" deserve, at the very least, less than "us"; "they" may even receive disregard or violence. Regardless of our moral stances regarding same-sex sex, Christians should be aware of and attentive to ways in which sexual others are at risk for cruelty, discrimination and violence.

New Patterns

While the homosexual–heterosexual binary is still useful at times, it is fading from use. I learned this the hard way, by embarrassing myself at school. Up until graduate school, I had used "homosexual" as a neutral catchall term for anyone who wasn't heterosexual, but I quickly learned that it was anything but neutral, and anything but accurate as a catchall. My fellow graduate student Rory Anderson and I did fieldwork at the Metropolitan Community Church of Washington, D.C. (MCCDC), a multiracial, middle-class gay-affirming church that was encouraging its members to move into the neighborhood and cultivate a residential community around the church. The neighborhood was already populated, however, mostly by low-income African Americans. Rory and I studied how sexuality and spirituality work together to influence people's understanding of "neighborhood," and how gay and lesbian Christians from MCCDC were mindful, or not, of low-income renters who might be displaced by their neighborhood redevelopment.

We wrote the first draft of the paper about *homosexuals*, but our advising professor corrected us. He rejected *homosexual* because of its roots in medical and religious discourse that casts homosexuals as deviant. A better term, he said, would be *queer*, which shocked me because in my Christian circles, *queer* was an insult. LGBT may also work well, he said, or LGBTQ, but we hadn't heard those acronyms used by people at MCCDC. In the end, Rory and I used *lesbian*, *gay* and *queer*, because those were the words our research participants used to describe themselves.[20]

Anthropologist Shaka McGlotten explains that these concerns are much more important than just word play.[21] They represent new patterns for understanding sexuality. Additive approaches (describing oneself as a white U.S. Christian able-bodied heterosexual, for example) emphasize the intersections between elements of identity vulnerable to discrimination: race, class, nationality, gender, age, ability, sexuality and so forth. Alphabetic approaches distinguish various sexualities with acronyms such as LGBT, LGBTQ, LGBTQQI (questioning, intersex) or, the lengthiest I've seen, LGBTQQPA(H), BDSM (lesbian, gay, bisexual, transgender, queer, questioning, pansexual, asexual, heterosexual, bondage, domination/discipline, submission, sadomasochism).[22]

The alphabetic approach is a helpful turn from "homosexual" because, in its use, those defined by a label are asserting self-definition. It moves beyond overgeneralizations that describe few people well. But these new patterns still rest upon the underlying belief that desire and identity are closely linked. Additionally, heterosexuality remains entrenched as a concept with the power of norming; that is, it sets the norm from which others depart, regardless of the labels used to describe the others. In this sense, the old cultural pattern is stable in continuing to bifurcate heterosexuals and all others, even while the "other" category has become more refined.

Newer Patterns

Increasingly, people are refusing to pick sexual identity categories for themselves.[23] Psychologist Lisa M. Diamond interviewed a number of same-sex-attracted women every few years for ten years, and in that time, more than two-thirds of the women in her study had changed their identity labels at least once, some more than once. Though all had some degree of same-sex attraction, some women shifted from calling themselves lesbian to calling themselves heterosexual; these women had fairly minimal same-sex attraction, or they were (or were likely to be) in relationships with men. Others shifted from bisexual to lesbian, from lesbian to bisexual, or from lesbian, bisexual or heterosexual to unlabeled.[24] "Unlabeled" women relied on either their gender (female) or their humanity to ground their sense of self.

Psychologist Mark Yarhouse and a team of researchers found results similar to Diamond's when they studied 104 Christian college sexual-minority students. Many of the college-age men and women in the study chose not to affiliate with a sexual identity label, or chose to change their labels over time. Yarhouse writes, "The commitment to an identity label may be falling off among sexual minority youth."[25]

This even newer pattern might be called a sexuality of speculation. McGlotten writes, "Speculation is a way of seeing critically,
awry or anew. . . . Seeing isn't always believing; rather, seeing is
also conceived as a sort of wondering."[26] She argues that the political and personal urgency of the issues surrounding sexuality
does not warrant exaggerated claims of sure and solid knowledge.
Instead, we should persist in speculation and wonder, watching for
exceptions, changes and surprises at least as much as for definitions and conclusions.

The Trouble with Homosexuality

Nineteenth-century sexual identity categories represent a modern
scientific effort to categorize (homosexual or heterosexual) and
evaluate (normal or abnormal, well or sick, respectable or deviant) human sexuality. This approach is played out. Many in our
society have moved on to newer patterns such as the additive or
alphabetic approaches, and even to rejections of sexual identity
labels altogether.

The trouble with homosexuality is that, for today's world, it is
an outdated, derisive way of describing people with same-sex
sexuality. "Homosexuality" as an identity category is not something that arrived in our world directly from creation (in which
case it would be good) nor directly from the Fall (in which case it
would be bad). Really, it came from nineteenth-century U.S.
medical researchers who were attempting to categorize people
whose sexuality deviated from a male-female, marital, procreative norm.

Sexual identity categories, however they are named, lay a grid of
meaning over our created nature as males and females and, even
more fundamentally, as humans. Being gay or straight is more
complex than just feeling certain feelings and then taking on the
social identity that matches the feelings. As crosscultural evidence
shows, sometimes sexual desire takes the lead in forming same-sex

relations, but other times gender performance, masculinity, femininity or even paid employment is the most important factor. Though many modern Western societies connect sexual desire directly to sexual identity, that's just one way of making sense of sexual feelings, and one way of establishing a social role. "Homosexuality" represents one way of linking together identity, feelings and behavior. But—whether we affirm or condemn it in practice— the concept itself paints the issue with too broad a brush.

Adding to the problem, Christianity too often offers a "one-size-fits-all" condemnation of homosexuality. It's no surprise that such ethereal ethics, mismatched with the culture into which they speak, are poorly accepted. Telling same-sex-attracted people to just stop sinning sexually often doesn't even make sense; it's like a missionary preaching in English to a non-English-speaking group, doggedly refusing to learn the local language. Doing theology and ethics without consideration for social construction is not only inaccurate, it is destructive. It hurts sexual minorities who are already discriminated against, and it hurts heterosexual Christians by supporting their collective delusion of moral superiority. Christians sometimes rush to make ethical judgments about elements of the world, too quickly assuming that something like sexual identity is fixed, inborn and present in Bible times in the same ways it's present today. Considering the social construction of sexual identity challenges those assumptions and changes our picture of sexuality.

God created sexuality. People created sexual identity. For Christians, developing ethical understandings is always a task of cultural construction, but grounding sexual ethics in our humanity more than in contemporary sexual identity categories would be a starting point closer to God's created order. Making this move comes at a cost to heterosexuals, however. It puts them in the game as players instead of umpires. If heterosexuals abandon or at least minimize the importance of the categories that empower them to think more highly of themselves than they ought, they just might find themselves in the same boat with those who have been seen as lowly, damaged or damned. When it comes to sex, there is no privileged, holy "we" and no sinful, troubled "them"; there's only us, each of whom finds both virtue and vice in sexuality.

4

The Promise
of Sexual Holiness

My heart is not proud, LORD,
my eyes are not haughty;
I do not concern myself with great matters
or things too wonderful for me.
But I have calmed myself
and quieted my ambitions.
I am like a weaned child with its mother;
like a weaned child I am content.

Israel, put your hope in the LORD
both now and forevermore.

PSALM 131

I loved nursing; my twins nursed for fourteen months, and my singleton for nineteen. It was clear when the time to wean Max (the singleton) had come. From about fifteen months until the time he was weaned, he couldn't sit still on my lap. If he was anywhere near the nursing position, he rooted as if desperately hungry. He asked to nurse when he was bored, when he wanted me off the phone, when he was hurt, when he hadn't seen me for a while, when he was tired, when he wanted to get my attention away from one of his siblings, and—I nearly forgot this one— when he was hungry. As an infant, milk was his only source of sustenance, but after he started eating hamburgers and pretzels, nursing took on a host of other meanings.

When Max was weaned he sat on my lap in a new way, as his older brothers had. Without the powerful draw to the breast, he could be still instead of rooting and clinging. And he faced away from me, instead of toward me. His sitting position mirrored how his whole life was reoriented, reaching out toward childhood instead of turning in toward infancy.

Weaning was difficult for all of us. Each of my boys easily favored food over milk to satisfy their hunger, but for years after they were weaned they continued to suck on fingers, pacifiers and shirt cuffs. For my part, I still sometimes find myself daydreaming about nursing, wanting to enjoy that special intimacy again, if only in memory. Even as I welcomed their healthy development, it was hard to see their interests expand beyond the shelter of my arms. But there was no way to hold onto it; nursing had to end, and we all had to grow up.

With respect to our topic, I'm suggesting that we wean ourselves from the pattern of this world, the sexual identity framework that limits our ability to be calm, mature and at peace about sexuality. Sexual identity categories keep us rooting after moral law and clinging to moral judgment. They hinder us from cultivating an ethos of calm and quiet around sexual issues in our Christian communities and lives. When we claim to know the full measure of a person on the basis of sexual desire or actions, we are concerning ourselves with matters too great for us. When we gird our own identities by maligning others, or judge our sexual identities or sex lives in comparison to others, we are seeing with haughty eyes. When we root after the wrong things, we miss the peace and rest of a mature relationship with God, and whether or not we intend to, we deny that peace to others.

Unpacking the Groceries

When a young child is weaned, she may move from her mother's breast (or a bottle) to a highchair at the kitchen table. This is a monumental transition, to be sure, but eventually she'll need to develop even more independence in adulthood as she chooses and prepares her own meals and cultivates relationships with the people who share her table. Weaning ourselves from sexual identity categories takes us beyond nursing and childhood (and extends the metaphor in Psalm 131 beyond early childhood) toward a place of greater maturity. Instead of relying on sexual identity categories to tell us who we are and what our sexuality means, we're invited to steward sexuality in a more careful way, perhaps even with the contentment and calm described in Psalm 131.

To illustrate this, I brought two brown paper bags filled with groceries to class one day and set them side by side on the table that usually holds my lecture notes. John, a student in my anthropology class, volunteered to be my conversation partner.

"Which bag would you choose?" I asked.

John played along. "I can't make an informed choice because I don't know what's in the bags, or why I'm choosing one."

"Could you say which is good and which is bad?"

"No," John said. "I need to see what's inside each one."

I turned the bags around to reveal that one was labeled "homosexuality" and one was labeled "heterosexuality."

"Let's try again, John. Which bag is good and which is bad?" I asked.

John paused and tentatively offered, "It's not that simple—there are good and bad elements to each, depending on the situation or the person."

"Well, then, which would you choose for yourself?"

A longer pause. "That's not a good question, Dr. Paris. In the real world, it's not as straightforward as picking a bag of groceries. It seems like some people aren't given a choice at all."

"John, you're not being very cooperative," I teased. "Try this one. Based on their labels, what can you tell me about the items in the bags?"

He was quick to retort, "I don't even know what's in the bags! How could I evaluate what I haven't even seen?"

Our conversation could have gone on and on like this, with me asking overly simplistic questions about a subject that John hadn't been given time or information to adequately understand. The mounting sense of frustration that he seemed to experience was precisely what I wanted the class to observe.

Michelle, another student, got mad at the bags. "I'm so sick of the way we talk about homosexuality in the church," she said. "We've got to get past the labels. The labels just put people down." I agreed, and added that labels also raise other people up. No matter how much we strive for equality, respect and compassion, the categories themselves perpetuate inequality and hierarchy.

The apostle Paul recognized how the patterns of the world tend to create hierarchies of human worth: "For by the grace given to me I say to everyone among you not to think of yourself more highly than you ought to think, but to think with sober judgment, each according to the measure of faith that God has assigned" (Romans 12:3 NRSV). Unpacking the groceries is an exercise in sober judgment (we could also call it honest self-evaluation or discernment). For some, it may lift them from moral degradation or even dehumanization toward equality; for others, it may chasten their sense of sexual moral superiority.

I began removing items from the grocery bags, cans and boxes relabeled with words such as *desire, fantasy, behaviors, relationships, memories, hopes, thoughts, health* and *marriage*. Without meaning to (it seemed), Michelle laughed a little.

"What is it, Michelle?" I asked.

"Well, your groceries are kind of hokey, but other than that, I get it! Just as it's impossible to judge an entire bag of groceries, it's

Figure 4.1

impossible to make a blanket statement about a person's sexuality. It's better to consider the specific parts of our sexualities and deal with them one by one."

"Right!" I exclaimed. "And the more seriously we take the specifics, the less we even need the bags."

For any given person in any given season of life, various elements of sexuality or clusters of elements may be placid, others active, and others troubled or even tormented. Viewed from the sexual identity perspective, a Christian "heterosexual" may seem to have godly sexuality. When their sexuality is unpacked, however, there may be important areas for healing or growth. The blanket statement that "heterosexuality is good" may even hinder this person from facing sexual struggles. On the flip side, in conservative settings a Christian "homosexual" may be written off as sinful or defective, though this person may have maturity and health in their sexuality that could benefit others.

Groceries can't be carried home one by one; at some point they need to be put in a bag. Similarly, the many elements of our human sexuality get gathered up—but they don't need to be separated into sexual identity categories; in my class exercise, the items in the "heterosexual" bag are identical to those in the "homosexual" bag. The elements of sexuality coalesce in our humanity. Sexuality is therefore better approached at the general level of humanity and the specific level of individuality, without the mediating level of sexual identity. We should all carry identical bags labeled "beloved," from which we unpack the unique elements of our sexual lives. (More on this in chapter five.)

Sexual Holiness

Sexual identity categories offer a shortcut for evaluating sexuality that doesn't devote proper attention to all the dimensions of human sexuality. It's the equivalent of buying groceries by the bag, instead of item by item. As a child matures toward food independence, she needs a method for choosing foods. That method may never be explicit, but she might use criteria such as taste, food quality, cost and her unique health concerns. To a certain extent, her choices will be like all other humans; we all need water and a supply of calories balanced between protein, fat, carbohydrates, vitamins and minerals. In other ways, her choices will be unique. She may need to accommodate diabetes or lactose-intolerance, for instance, or may want to gain or lose weight. She might prefer rice over potatoes, or lamb over beef, depending on how she was raised.

Sexual holiness is an approach for making sober judgments about sexuality. In describing sexual holiness, I borrow from the

Holiness tradition (since it's their name, surely they've developed a good definition!). John Wesley described holiness as love of God and neighbor, which is Jesus' description of the greatest commandment (Matthew 22:34-40). Wesleyan theologian Mildred Wynkoop says Wesley's theology of love was less about systematic or dogmatic conclusions and more about the dynamics of a personal relationship with God: "Holiness is love locked into the True Center, Jesus Christ our Lord. Being 'true,' all of the self—and progressively all of life—comes into harmony and wholeness and strength."[1]

When distorted, holiness is used as a synonym for morality, when really it's about being more and more in love with God and with humanity. In the area of sexuality, specifically, sexual morality too easily becomes an idol, whether it's premarital virginity, marital chastity or heterosexuality. People follow hard after it, measure their worth by it and are sometimes devastated when they offend it. Moreoever, Christians teach others to measure their worth by morality rather than by their belovedness. When sexual morality is elevated to an idolatrous place, it diminishes people's sense of being loved and being able to love, instead of being put in its place by love.

Being a lover, in the fullest sense, is an important part of human sexuality. When we pursue sexual holiness, we seek to give and receive love with God and with other people in and through our sexuality. Love draws us toward morality and right behavior, but it doesn't demand that we do the right thing for the wrong reason, such as repressing or expressing sexuality in a "Christian" way for fear of hell or for need of approval from other Christians.

In post–sexual identity Christian communities, sexual holiness becomes a common standard for all believers. Same-sex attraction and behavior still matter, but not as identity-constituting characteristics and not as points of theological disagreement that warrant separation or exclusion. Instead of a few sexual behaviors being selected for elevated judgment, all elements of human sexuality become part of the mix, shaping what it means for each person to be holy in their sexuality. Sexual holiness encompasses the sexual identity framework, thereby diminishing its importance in light of a more important biblical value. Some individuals or communities may discard sexual identity categories altogether in the way they think of themselves, describe themselves to others and talk within particular communities. Others may retain the categories for strategic purposes but no longer mistake them as timeless, universally true or biblical. Like my GPA, sexual identity categories can become our servants instead of our masters.

Dimensions of Sexual Holiness

Academics and church leaders from a broad range of Holiness churches formed the Wesleyan Holiness Study Project, a group committed to working across denominational lines to communicate the message of holiness to contemporary audiences both within and beyond Holiness churches.[2] (My personal affiliations are both within and beyond the Holiness tradition. I worshiped at a Church of God [Anderson] for four years and was married in that church, and now am part of the Brethren in Christ denomination, which has Mennonite and Wesleyan roots.) *The Holiness Manifesto,* a public statement

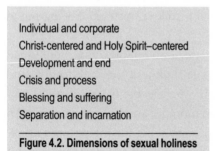

Individual and corporate
Christ-centered and Holy Spirit–centered
Development and end
Crisis and process
Blessing and suffering
Separation and incarnation

Figure 4.2. Dimensions of sexual holiness

that emerged from the project, describes a number of dimensions of holiness, each of which contains contrasting or even paradoxical elements. Applying these dimensions to sexuality (I selected those that best apply) demonstrates the richness of holiness.

   1. *Individual and corporate.* Christians are called to holiness in all areas of life, both personal and corporate. Personal sexual holiness includes how a person cares for his or her sexual feelings, thoughts and actions. In the next chapters, I'll offer my view of what sexual holiness may mean for both sexual activity and celibacy. My views are conservative—I'm a "sex only within marriage between a man and a woman" kind of Christian—but I am well aware that Christians of good faith disagree about the meaning of personal sexual holiness.[3] Maligning those with whom we disagree, even to the point of questioning the validity of their faith or salvation, is counterproductive and damages the witness of our religion as a whole, which is supposed to be comprised of believers from many times and places united in their devotion to Jesus, not to a set of beliefs about sexuality.

While sexuality is personal in many ways, it also is a matter of public, corporate concern. Christians have done well in promoting healing around some issues of sexual brokenness. One example is in the area of sex trafficking, which Christians, along with people of other religions and perspectives, are working to eliminate. International Justice Mission, a Christian nonprofit organization, is particularly devoted to this, working around the world to address human rights violations, including sex trafficking.[4] Others work to reduce sexual abuse when they require background checks for church workers and establish grievance procedures in churches and denominations. On matters of general consensus, such as sex trafficking, rape, abuse, addictions and breaches of marriage, Christians contribute well to the public good, even partnering with individuals or groups with whom they may disagree on other issues.

When it comes to contentious sexual issues, however, Christian public engagement becomes more, well, contentious. Within the United States, there's no consensus on issues like abortion, teen access to contraception, sex education in public schools, obscenity laws for media, sexuality-based hate-crime classifications, health insurance for domestic partnerships, gay marriage, and discrimination in employment or housing based on sexual identity. Internationally, Christians hold vastly different beliefs about polygamy, female circumcision, the value of an infertile wife, the propriety of birth control, patriarchy, and even domestic abuse (some would encourage an abused woman to leave and find safety, while others would distort Scripture, instructing her to win over her abuser in "quietness and full submission" [1 Timothy 2:11]).[5] Sometimes Christians adopt the worst political strategies: shouting, bullying, demonizing the opposition, refusing to listen and even becoming violent. Despite the urgency of many of these matters, homosexuality, in particular, has become the trigger issue over which believers break fellowship with each other. The world in which Christians all agree about sexual issues is an imaginary one. Love of God and neighbor, the heart of holiness, has to be practiced in the real world in the midst of these disagreements.

2. Christ-centered and Holy Spirit–centered. "The Holy Spirit's work within us leads us to conformity to the person of Jesus Christ. Neither should be expressed without the other."[6] When the Holy Spirit (or a particular representation of the Holy Spirit) is emphasized to the exclusion of Christ, sexual holiness can be misconstrued as whatever seems right or feels right to a person. "Healthy" sexuality may become a substitute for holiness, and acceptance or affirmation may become more important than redemption and sanctification. For example, a progressive Christian group states, "All persons have the right and responsibility to lead sexual lives that express love, justice, mutuality, commitment, consent and pleasure. Grounded in respect for the body and for the vulnerability that intimacy brings, this ethic fosters physical, emotional and spiritual health."[7] While this progressive vision encompasses many elements of justice, such as reducing sexual abuse and violence, it relies on a general value of "spiritual health" that neglects more specific and distinctive elements of the Christian tradition. On the other hand, when Jesus (or a particular representation of Jesus) is emphasized over the Holy Spirit, Christians can coerce themselves and others into behavioral compliance with Jesus' moral teachings to the neglect of cultivating personal spirituality and conscience.

Centering holiness in both the person of Christ and the work of the Holy Spirit is the path of costly discipleship, as Dietrich Bonhoeffer described: "Grace is costly because it compels a man to submit to the yoke of Christ and follow him; it is grace because Jesus says: 'My yoke is easy and my burden is light'"[8] Costly discipleship avoids, on the one hand, cheap grace that permits moral excess, and on the other hand, rigid moralism that occludes mercy and joy.

3. Development and end. The "end" of a holy life is to be like Christ. When it comes to sexual holiness, however, the end is often misperceived as a life station (heterosexual marriage) instead of a quality of life (Christlikeness). For some, marriage is not a viable or even a desirable state. And for some, the same is true of heterosexuality.

The "end" of life is to be holy, but the development of holiness never ends. It's just as important, therefore, to emphasize Christlikeness in the *development* of a spiritual life, not just as the end. It can be tempting to judge a person's present state in terms of an ideal future state, which isn't right; in fact, it's haughty. Sober judgment allows room for each person to develop over time, and for others to understand that person's current context, history and future hopes.

On the corporate level, it's important to encourage the development of institutions and traditions. As its failure to protect children from priests' abuse is exposed, the Roman Catholic Church today, for example, is hopefully developing institutional holiness—policies and processes that protect vulnerable people. For Protestants, it seems that even when groups who disagree—like Lutherans and Anglicans over homosexuality—succeed in securing the "end," or the theological position, they desire, the process itself too often compromises Christian unity and mutual respect.

Christians in societies that rely on sexual identity social constructs tend to read those constructs back into Scripture, and this has ramifications for both personal and corporate dimensions of life. It can seem as though there are just five or six passages directed at homosexuals (portions of Leviticus 18 and 20; Romans 1; 1 Corinthians 6; 1 Timothy 1 and a few others), and that the Bible's primary message to those with same-sex sexuality is that they are abominable sinners. Even those who affirm same-sex sexuality sometimes focus on reinterpreting these passages to the exclusion of broader biblical themes about human identity, sexuality and family. On a corporate level, this leads to institutions using theological positions on homosexuality as boundary markers for membership or even salvation, or as indicators of other beliefs about the Bible, Jesus, morality or politics.

4. Crisis and process. Salvation is described by some in crisis terms: at a low point in life, a person received Christ and received instantaneous transformation. Others describe it as a process, perhaps not remembering a single moment of receiving Christ; since birth or early childhood, their life with God has been unfolding.

With respect to stewardship of our sexual lives, some elements of sexuality may change instantaneously through religious experiences such as prayer, or through effort of the will, or through life changes such as marriage. Other times, change happens more slowly as part of an embedded process. After sexual trauma such as assault, for instance, a person may find healing in their emotions, which links to their relationships, which links to behaviors, thoughts and feelings. Still other times, sexuality doesn't change much at all.

Similarly, on a corporate level a church or Christian community may announce a new, large-scale turn of direction, a "crisis" of sorts. People could begin supporting sexual justice for those involved in global sex trafficking, for instance, or launch a new commitment to local service. That same church or community, however, may have informal social norms that make celibate people feel second-class. Changing patterns of communication, socializing and perceiving each other can be an incremental process. As with individuals, holiness develops simultaneously as crisis and process in institutions.

5. Blessing and suffering. Loving Jesus means receiving many blessings, but also sharing in Christ's sufferings. Some Christians use the sexual identity framework to argue that heterosexuals are blessed, and homosexuals (and all other non-heterosexuals) are suffering (and if they seem to be happy or thriving, they're really suffering deep down inside). Others use the same framework with a different interpretation, believing that both heterosexuals and homosexuals (and all other sexual identities) are blessed. The suffering that occurs in one's sexuality, then, is often attributed to societal or family disapproval. Still others seem to see all human sexuality as fraught with suffering, and are reluctant to celebrate sexuality as one of God's good gifts.

Unpacking the groceries makes this tension abundantly clear. When sexuality is seen in all its dimensions, it is evident that, regardless of their sexual orientation or identity, many people experience both blessing and suffering over time, and perhaps even simultaneously. A person may have a strong marriage with an enjoyable sexual relationship, but be suffering in their physical sexual health. Another person may have tension or even torment about their sexual behaviors at present, but may have peace in their memories of the past and in their hopes for the future. Remembering that Jesus experienced both blessing and suffering can help remind us to expect both in our sexual lives.

6. Separation and incarnation. With respect to the world, holiness requires separation at times and, at other times, meaningful, redemptive engagement. A Christian may seek to be at the same time separate from the world in some ways and deeply engaged in other ways. We can work toward holiness by making cultural engagement thoughtful, aware, intentional and justice-oriented, and move away from that which is selfish, thoughtless or hurtful to others.

Holiness in Community

Taken together, these dimensions clarify the meaning of holiness as a quality of life shared by all believers. With respect to homosexuality, sexual holiness doesn't boil down the matter to the single question, "Is it a sin?" It honors the importance of this question and the necessity of answering it, but at the same time it recognizes that people and groups will answer it differently. Holiness also doesn't boil down the complexities of human sexuality to a list of moral rules. It's not that rules are wrong or entirely unimportant, but they are less important than the believer's discernment that stems from a transformed mind.

Throughout the apostle Paul's teachings, including earlier chapters in Romans, Paul tells followers of Christ that they do not need to follow Old Testament law. Jesus fulfilled the law by getting to the heart of the matter, the human heart. When followers of Jesus worship truly (or "spiritually" or "reasonably," from Romans 12:1), they don't just follow a new law (the law of Paul, or the law of religious conservatism or liberalism). They cultivate inner transformation that empowers each person to make sober judgments about what is good, acceptable and perfect. Sexual holiness, then, isn't as simple as a list of do's and don'ts (a new law), nor is it as open-ended as affirming "healthy" sexuality, however a person may define it.

The renewed mind of the believer flourishes in community. Romans 12:1-2 is written in the plural, addressing individuals gathered together in the church, and the chapter moves immediately to the metaphor of the body of Christ in which each person plays a vital part. In the class in which John and Michelle were students (a

Christian college class is one kind of Christian community), the nuances and tensions of sexual holiness provided a better framework for sex and gender issues than the sexual identity framework. Over the course of the class, we discussed a variety of topics. One was heterosexual body modification (makeup, weight lifting, cosmetic surgery, weight loss, fashion and so on) as a strategy for attracting a mate. It became evident that while the cultivation of personal beauty may be an end for which humans were created, we often pursue that end with destructive means. We also viewed a documentary, and admired the nonprofit organization in Thailand it was on that rescues sex trafficking victims and works to prevent children from being sold into slavery. We were reminded that sexual holiness is corporate, public and global, not just a private dimension of our personal lives. In addition, we analyzed media (images and, when relevant, videos and lyrics) from celebrities including Al Green, Beyoncé, Victoria Beckham and Lady Gaga. The tension between separation and incarnation provided a framework for discussing when, and for what reasons, to consume secular media, and what kinds of engagement make a redemptive difference.

Conclusion

Perhaps it's no coincidence that nursing often has a depressing effect on the female sex drive, while weaning enlivens it. Weaning marks a transition in the woman's investment of her energy and body, particularly her breasts, in gestating and nursing her infant, and frees her to return to her husband. Similarly, weaning ourselves from sexual identity categories transitions Christians from investing energy in moralizing and making divisions among believers toward really pursuing sexual holiness in our own lives and in the world.

Adam and Eve ate from the tree of the knowledge of good and evil, which was knowledge too great for them. We're like Adam and Eve when we get life from our knowledge of good and evil, setting ourselves as judge of others and of ourselves.[9] Maybe human sexuality isn't created to be a place of fulfillment or perfection, but one of rest and calm. When hope is placed in God, instead of in getting it right, we can be like a quiet child on a mother's lap. The peace and stillness doesn't come from being perfect, but from loving and being loved by God and neighbor.

In the post–sexual identity church, there's no moral high ground for heterosexuals and no closet for homosexuals. There's just people, each of whom is lover and loved.

Sexual Desire Is
(Not) a Big Deal

Sexual desire causes problems for people. A wife has strong sexual desire, but for someone other than her husband. A husband takes a medication that erases his libido. An engaged couple commits to abstinence, but desire gets the better of them. A Christian with same-sex attraction believes her desires conflict with God's intent for her life. Another Christian with same-sex attraction has no problem with his desires, but feels hurt by his religion that condemns what he experiences as a blessing.

Sexual desire causes problems for religion too. In many of its cultural and historical contexts, Christianity seems to find—or perhaps create—a tormented relationship with sexual desire. Many Christians today downplay the importance of feelings in general, including sexual ones. Sometimes faith is even defined as the opposite of feelings; regardless of what you feel, you ought to believe and have faith. In this view, feelings are denigrated as fickle and subjective, and faith is esteemed as stable and objective. When applied to sexuality, this view encourages people to pay little attention to sexual desire, and to focus instead on correct behavior and belief. At the same time, however, Christians have bought into the idea that sexual desire is an indicator of sexual identity. As a result, Christians often encourage and even harangue people into changing their sexual feelings in order to change their sexual identity. In this view, it seems that while feelings may often be ignored or repressed in favor of "faith," when it comes to sexual feelings, believers need to toe the line.

If sexuality is like groceries, then sexual desire is a single can or box. One item cannot accurately indicate the meaning or value of the entire bag. But if we as Christians are going to abstain from linking sexual feelings directly to identity, then we need to generate new ways (or, better yet, rejuvenate old ways) of understanding desire, identity and the relationship between them. Sexual holiness is an invitation to renew our stewardship of sexuality by first viewing human beings as beloved. This view of identity beckons us to treat sexual desire with care, instead of badgering it with judgment, repression or cure.

You Are What You Want?

My student Gregory knew he was gay long before he ever had sex with another man. For as far back as he could remember, he had always and only been attracted to males. Years before any same-sex behavior, the feelings themselves made him question his sexual identity and eventually come out as gay. In young adulthood, this choice resulted in untenable compartmentalization; he split his time, on a daily basis, between a Christian college campus with a chaste student culture and local gay bars that were anything but chaste. Moreover, at the same time he was disappointing himself with sexual promiscuity, he was working hard to cultivate a relationship with God and to understand what Scripture and the church really meant to him. The sexual identity framework did solve one problem—it helped him find an identity label, social role and community that made sense of his sexuality—but it caused a number of others.

Whether it is homosexuality, heterosexuality, LGTBQ or another variation, the sexual identity framework is always limited because it selects certain elements of sexuality as identity-constituting and downplays other important dimensions. Consider the wife with sexual desire for a man other than her husband, or the husband whose libido disappeared. These desires may cause great distress and even alter the course of a marriage, but they don't change the sexual identities of the people involved. Or consider Gregory: he wants lots of things, sexually speaking. He desires intimacy in a monogamous relationship. He desires the ability to change his pattern of meaningless hookups. He wants God to guide his relationships. But the sexual identity framework fixates on who Gregory wants to have sex with, and offers him a corresponding identity and community; it highlights only the "sexual object choice" and labels people accordingly. The rest of a person's desires—which are sometimes the stronger parts, such as religious devotion or marital commitment—are neglected.

Additionally, the sexual identity framework unnecessarily separates people from others. For example, it seems to me that Gregory and I have a lot in common, even in our sexualities. I may be older, female and married, but I share with him the desire to let God into every part of my life, to be monogamous, to be loved and appreciated, and to find the power to change the troublesome parts of my life. In terms of religion, as well, Gregory and I have similarities. We're both part of a local Christian community (our college) and the broader Christian tradition, and we share religious understandings and practices. But sexual identity—my heterosexuality no less than his homosexuality—gets in the way.

When it comes to sexual identity, Christians generally rely on the same cultural logic as others: people identify with sexual identity categories based on their feelings. The only difference is that the church adds a layer of morality. In conservative churches, for instance, one sexual identity category is right and all others are wrong. This framework puts same-sex-attracted believers in an impossible situation. They can leave the church and comfortably live out their sexuality, which is a dire option for committed Christians. Or they can remain in the church and either attempt to become heterosexual (which I

explore in further depth below), or remain non-heterosexual in the
church as a second-class citizen. As long as heterosexuality is the
prize, people of same-sex attraction and/or behavior will never be
able to win. One gay Christian man told me about how hard he
struggled to live a celibate life in faithfulness to his understanding of
Scripture. In the eyes of many in his church, he had moved out of the
"gay" category and into the "young adult singles" group—but it
seemed that there too, without marriage, he still was incomplete and
deficient. Other churches, of course, affirm same-sex sexuality; this
choice has different consequences but relies on the same method,
layering morality on top of preexisting cultural categories.

In my class on women's spiritual experiences, students spoke of
homosexuals as "them," people outside the fold and certainly outside our classroom. Gregory said to me privately, "The *them* is *me*.
It's hard not to take offense at the things people say." I wasn't surprised, then, when he responded to my ideas about dismantling
the sexual identity framework with this note: "As for your philo-
sophical/theological discussion of homosexuality, I thought it was
interesting. However, being a twenty-first-century person, I find
that sexual orientation *is* an identity factor. I have to accept that I
exist in a particular place and time." He's right; people need identity categories that give a sense of self and community. I'm not
criticizing Gregory for conforming to the pattern of this world, because Christians haven't offered an alternative.

You Are Beloved

A Christian view might make different sense of wanting and of being. What you want is not a message about who you are. Human
identity links directly to God, the creation to its Creator. From
beginning to end, Scripture persuades us that we are God's beloved. The first mention of humans, in the first creation narrative,
asserts the likeness between humans and their Creator: "So God
created human beings in his own image, in the image of God he

created them; male and female he created them" (Genesis 1:27). The prophet Isaiah picks up on this creation theme, saying, "He who created you, Jacob, he who formed you, Israel: 'Do not fear, for I have redeemed you; I have summoned you by name; you are mine'" (Isaiah 43:1). And while Jesus' life and teachings contain myriad instances of love for people, my favorite is from the beginning of his public ministry, when Jesus was healing and teaching people in various towns. Matthew writes in his Gospel, "When he saw the crowds, he had compassion on them, because they were harassed and helpless, like sheep without a shepherd" (9:36). Whether humans are brand new in the Garden of Eden, or poor, sick and politically dominated in the Roman Empire, God responds to us with compassion and love.

The sexual identity framework labels the grocery bag "lesbian," "bisexual" or some other category based on the condition of a single item, desire. If "beloved" were the label on every bag, then identity would be secure, regardless of the items in the bag or their condition. Sexual desire may be simple, complicated, distorted or confused, and when desire is troubled, it is a very serious matter for the person experiencing it. But no matter the condition of our desire, the identity category is still "beloved human being."

Desire (in general, not just sexual) is multifaceted. Even within the same person, desire can be very bad, very good or conflicted. When sexual desire goes bad, the results can be disastrous. When David followed his desire for Bathsheba, for example, two marriages were damaged and Bathsheba's husband was killed (2 Samuel 11). Shechem the son of Hamor followed his desire for Dinah and raped her (Genesis 34). James offers the direst warning about the danger of desire: "But each of you is tempted when you are dragged away by your own evil desire and enticed. Then, after desire has conceived, it gives birth to sin; and sin, when it is full-grown, gives birth to death" (1:14-15). Sinful desire can link to identity in destructive ways. For example, Shechem's sexual desire seems to have fortified his gender identity such that he used his superior physical strength to dominate Dinah.

When desire is good, however, it is very good. The Psalms describe how God delights in fulfilling human desires: "You [God] open your hand and satisfy the desires of every living thing" (145:16). Sexual desire can be very good as well. The lovers in Song of Solomon go on and on about sexual desire, and it's a beautiful thing: "I belong to my beloved, and his desire is for me" (7:10). Fulfilled sexual desire may bring pleasure, comfort, intimacy, joy and babies. And desire can bolster human identity in positive ways, such as when sexual desire leads a person to assume social roles such as husband, wife or parent.

Of course, it's rarely so simple to label desire "good" or "bad"; often, desires are conflicted. Paul highlights this tension in Romans 7:18 where he says, "For I have the desire to do what is good, but I cannot carry it out." This is often true of sexual desire as well. Like Gregory wanting monogamy but practicing promiscuity, people genuinely want to do what is good, but find themselves doing something else, or they genuinely want to want what is good, but instead want something else. This tendency toward conflict and unpredictability is one reason why desire is not reliable as a bestower of identity. Part of working out our salvation is waiting for God, "who is at work in [us], enabling [us] both to will and to work for his good pleasure" (Philippians 2:13 NRSV). One of the paradoxes of holiness is that it is both development and end; the perfection of the will, or desire, is always a work in progress. Therefore desire, even sexual desire, is a venue for grace.

When desire is seen as the sun around which identity orbits, both become rigid and unassailable; to question desire is to question a person's selfhood and worth. However, when desire is seen as a shifting planet that moves around the stable sun of belovedness, one's identity as a child of God can remain in place regardless of how desire changes (or doesn't change). And when desire is re-

spected as a site of conflict and a venue for grace,
sponsive to discernment and care—though this may or ma͏̈,
mean that desire will respond to attempts to change it, as Paul lamented poignantly in Romans 7.

Is Change Possible?

Because Christians have bought into the sexual identity framework, many have developed an unhealthy obsession with changing sexual orientation. When it comes to certain sins, say gossip or mean-spiritedness or grudge-holding, we are often satisfied if a person minimizes them. There are no therapy programs devoted specifically to eradicating the impulse to gossip, for instance, and people don't devote months or years of their lives exclusively to converting mean-spiritedness into kindness. Even in the area of sexuality, attempts to change most unwanted sexual desires—say, desire for someone other than one's spouse, or a desire to avoid sex with one's spouse—aren't used as the measure of a person's spirituality or identity. Even when taken very seriously, these problems are considered part of the human condition; a person isn't expected to make them disappear altogether (though if God should make a dramatic change, such grace would be welcome).

But when it comes to same-sex attraction, people devote months and years to therapeutic and spiritual programs that promise to eradicate or redirect not only same-sex behavior but also same-sex feelings. What's ironic is that even though changing sexual desire may seem to be a thoroughly Christian approach, it often eclipses other biblical teachings about desire: that it is fickle, often conflicted and, even for devout believers, not always under our control. Desire itself illustrates the paradox of crisis and process existing simultaneously in the Christian life.

Attempts to change sexual desire are just that: interventions focused on feelings and behaviors. When desire is uncoupled from identity, we can consider the question of change in a more straight-

forward way. In this view, the work doesn't impact human identity; whether or not a person succeeds in changing their sexuality,
their identity as a beloved creation of God is intact.

Change through reparative therapy. Reparative therapy is a
general term for a variety of interventions that seek to "repair" a
person's sexual behaviors, orientation or feelings. Most reparative
therapists are Christian, and many rely on Elizabeth Moberly's
theory that same-sex attraction is rooted in family dysfunction,
specifically deficits in a person's relationship with their same-sex
parent.[1] Many same-sex-attracted Christians who have tried to
change their orientation through a ministry, therapy or residential
program have relied on this model.

Jeanette Howard, a central figure in the ex-gay movement, wrote
a testimonial book, *Out of Egypt*, about how reparative therapy
helped her triumph over lesbianism. More than ten years later, she
wrote another book in which she states,

> Certainties that I held, back in the late 1980s, regarding sex-
> ual "healing" have become less certain and less static in na-
> ture. . . . Despite all my efforts, prayer, application and ser-
> vice, I had to admit that I had not travelled along a continuum
> and entered the world of heterosexuality. . . . Despite joining
> a Christian dating agency and opening myself up to many
> avenues of experience, I could not honestly see myself ever
> committing to a man. It was time to own the truth.[2]

She describes the pressure she felt, in the Christian limelight, to
claim "victory" over sin and to promote the belief that heterosexuality is possible for devout same-sex-attracted Christians who try
hard enough. Today, she is one of many who acknowledge that
change is not always possible, and it's never easy.

Christian psychologists Mark Yarhouse and Stanton Jones sub-
jected stories like this to scientific scrutiny in their study on the
experiences of ninety-eight people, many of whom were Christians,

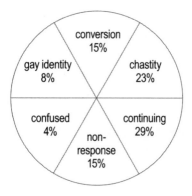

Figure 5.1. Sexual orientation change through therapy

who were highly committed to changing their sexual orientation through religiously mediated interventions.[3] These approaches could include prayer, worship, small groups, therapy or other programs. Yarhouse and Jones reported their results in six categories:

- conversion (15 percent): the person reports "considerable resolution of homosexual orientation issues and substantial conversion to heterosexual attraction"

- chastity (23 percent): the person's same-sex attractions are reduced or gone, and in a way that no longer causes distress

- continuing (29 percent): the person may have experienced reduced same-sex attraction, but the person remains committed to changing more

- non-response (15 percent): the person has experienced no significant change in orientation

- confused (4 percent): the person experienced no change, and has given up on trying to change, but hasn't embraced a gay identity

- gay identity (8 percent): the person has given up on change and has embraced a gay identity

These results may seem promising or disappointing, depending on your perspective. To their secular colleagues in the American Psychological Association, Yarhouse and Jones insist that therapeutic attempts to change sexual orientation can work and do not harm the participants. Compared to other therapeutic outcomes, a 15 percent success rate is not poor (success could be as high as 38 percent if conversion and chastity are both considered successful outcomes). But to their fellow Christians, including Christian psychologists who practice reparative therapy, they deliver sobering news: it just isn't realistic to tell a same-sex-attracted person that they can surely resolve their struggles through therapy. In fact, it's more realistic to tell them that, while their particular future can't be predicted, the statistical likelihood is that at least some degree of same-sex attraction will remain.

Instead of relying on either cynical pessimism (sexual identity never changes) or arrogant optimism (anyone can change if they try hard enough), Yarhouse encourages Christians toward realistic biblical hope. He believes that "focusing on identity can have a profound impact on a person's life, regardless of whether (or the degree to which) attractions or orientation changes."[4] Therapy may be helpful for some. For others, though, it can be a reinforcement of the cultural lie that what you want is who you are in that it's just trying to get people to want the right things instead of the wrong things, so they can then be good instead of bad.

Change through sexual fluidity. But aren't there plenty of examples of people changing sexual orientation? I was surprised to learn that, for my students, change is expected. In one class, a lesbian guest speaker told her life story: always attracted to women, she married a man out of duty and raised a family with him. In the 1960s, she left her husband for a woman and remains in a committed relationship with her to this day. After she left, I asked for feedback.

A student said, "I was surprised. She's, like, really a lesbian!"

"What do you mean?" I asked. "Of course she's a lesbian."

The student explained that, in her middle school and high school, kids "become gay" to be experimental, to get attention or to fit in with a certain group. Thus, even when it is grounded in genuine sexual feelings, homosexuality doesn't always stick; the feelings could change. It seems that, for this generation of students, what's surprising is that sexual orientation could be so permanent, not the fact that it fluctuates.

In different ways for different people, sexual feelings flex over time and across situations. Most research on homosexuality has been based on men, and in general, it seems that men have a higher proportion of genetic influence on sexual orientation. This has contributed to the misimpression that sexual orientation is entirely or almost entirely fixed at birth or in early childhood, and that changes in sexual orientation are merely developmental confusions or experimentations along the way to a truly permanent sexuality. More women, however, (and some men as well) seem to have a higher proportion of environmental influence, making their sexuality flex in response to situations.[5]

Psychologist Lisa M. Diamond (discussed in chapter three) was interested specifically in whether changes in sexuality were just transitional—phases along the way to a permanent sexuality—or whether something more substantial was happening.[6] Within the first two years of her ten-year study interviewing same-sex-attracted women, 30 percent of her subjects changed sexual identities. Most changed from "unlabeled" to lesbian or bisexual, but others changed from lesbian or bisexual to unlabeled, and still others became heterosexual. Some of those who became heterosexual were even disappointed; they would have rather remained lesbian or bisexual, but the strength and frequency of their same-sex attraction had lessened. Based on other studies, men show some flexibility, especially in response to opportunity or environmental constraint, but male sexuality seems to be fixed earlier in life (studies show this for animals as well as for humans).[7]

Diamond, Baumeister (his research was described in chapter two) and others agree that sexual orientation is a mix of genetics and environment, and that the mix is different for different people and changes over time. Diamond describes women of same-sex orientation who, in particular situations, fell in love with men. Likewise, a heterosexual woman may, in a particular situation, find herself attracted to a woman, even without meaning to be. Diamond's research is on sexual minority women, so these claims about sexual fluidity may be stronger for these women than for heterosexual women; further research remains to be done. But her point is sound: sexual orientation is not just a genetic given, nor is it just a lifestyle choice.

Frustrating for Christians wishing to change sexual orientation, this kind of change—sexual fluidity—is the easiest. It just happens, sometimes even to the surprise or dismay of the person experiencing it. Sexual fluidity does not, however, imply control over sexual desire. Some people experience genuine change in the direction of their sexual desire because of therapeutic work, others experience change through no effort of their own, and others experiment with change for a variety of reasons. This doesn't, however, mean that any person seeking to change their sexual orientation will be able to do so.

Deep change: Repentance. Early in his public ministry, Jesus announced, "The time has come. . . . The kingdom of God has come near. Repent and believe the good news!" (Mark 1:15). The Greek *metanoia*, translated "repent," pairs two words that mean "after" and "thinking or perceiving." Repentance is an "afterthought," a change of mind that is different from the earlier thought. As a child, I would have interpreted Jesus' message to mean, "I'm here now, so stop sinning and believe the good news!" I took repentance to mean a change of behavior away from sin. True repentance certainly includes a change of behavior, but its deeper meaning is a transformation of the mind. In this sense, Jesus' message harmonizes with Romans 12, calling people to be renewed by the transforming of their minds.

If, with respect to same-sex attraction, repentance is taken to mean fixing, curing or eliminating problematic desires, it seems that only some people will be able to follow Jesus' teaching. Yet, though some people may be able to change their sexual desire and others may not, all of us are called to repent: to change our minds in light of Jesus' good news. In this sense, repentance is less about fixing or curing, and more about a reorientation of perspective. With sexual desire, in particular, two repentances are in order: a turn from judgment to discernment and from cure to care.

From judgment to discernment. Some Christians cultivate an adversarial relationship with their sexuality: you are the judge and your sexuality is the offender (potential or actual). Judging involves adjudicating, making authoritative conclusions and even doling out punishments. At best, the judge may implement restorative justice, seeking to rehabilitate. More often, perhaps, the judge turns merciless, using retributive justice to punish with little regard for restoration. When sexuality is put on trial, no wonder it goes into hiding. It may seem moral to put away sin—stuff it away, ignore it, punish or shame it—but this is the kind of morality John Wesley warned against in his teachings on holiness. Morality divorced from discipleship and love is "holding to the outward form of godliness but denying its power" (2 Timothy 3:5 NRSV).

Other Christians judge sexuality positively. For example, the "Statement of Purpose" of the Metropolitan Community Churches, a denomination founded in part to affirm people of same-sex sexuality, states, "We believe that even in our humanness, we are holy. We are liberated from other people's definitions of who we are. We are made both body and spirit. We believe that our sexuality is a holy gift from God so we no longer distance our bodies from our experience with God."[8] In this view, held more widely than just in this denomination, because sexuality was created by God, it is holy "as is." I've worshiped at an MCC church and I respect their compassionate care for people who have been mistreated in other churches, but all-encompassing affirmation is very similar to the adversarial approach to sexuality. Though here, the judge absolves the defendant, in both cases judgments have been made. In place of discipleship, the adversarial approach offers morality and the inclusive approach offers affirmation. In both approaches a person can cling to these outward forms of godliness but deny the real power of holiness.

Discernment, on the other hand, involves real understanding. To discern something is to observe it, perceive it and figure it out. Discerning also involves assessing right and wrong, but in a way that includes a deep understanding of a person and their history, not a quick bang of the gavel. Instead of judge to offender, the relationship between a person and their sexuality becomes one of student and teacher. Each person's sexual journey tells a story, and we can learn to pay close attention and glean its lessons through sober judgment.

Discernment may be practiced through prayer, reflection or conversation with friends, and at times with therapy. Christian psychologists Mark Yarhouse and Warren Throckmorton are leaders in replacing reparative therapy with therapeutic approaches that point people toward values coherence.[9] First, they break down sexual identity into three components: attraction, orientation and identity. Sexual attractions are feelings, desires, longings or arousals. Sexual orientation is the dominant direction of sexual attractions, whether toward those of the same sex, other sex, both or neither. Sexual identity is a chosen social label that corresponds (or doesn't correspond) with attraction or orientation.

Instead of assuming that sexual desire links directly to identity, this model introduces several pauses, or moments for discernment. If a person feels same-sex attraction, what does it mean? For one person, it might be a one-time situation in the context of a particular relationship. For another, it might be related to family dynamics. For another, it might be lifelong and persistent. It's up to the person to make meaning of those feelings and to decide how desire ought to shape behavior. He may not assess the feelings as strong and persistent enough to label them an "orientation." Or he may, in which case he then needs to consider which sexual identity label, if any, he wishes to adopt, and what it will mean for him. This approach encourages sober judgment as a person identifies sexual feelings, clarifies personal values, makes meaning of both and makes choices about how to live.

This wisdom is not just for the same-sex attracted, however. Adopting the label "heterosexual" (or, more likely, falling into it by default) can be a way to avoid listening to what one's own sexuality may be saying. Because the direction of their sexuality seems to satisfy God's law, heterosexuals, it seems, can establish secure identity with reference to the law, not God's grace; as Jesus said, "It is not the healthy who need a doctor, but the sick" (Matthew 9:12). But in truth, heterosexual sexual journeys are complicated too, with feelings, thoughts, behaviors, relationships and values that don't line up perfectly.

In contrast to judgment that assesses a person's sexuality as good or bad, discernment honors the paradoxical way that blessing and suffering coexist in a holy life. Though sexual attractions and behaviors will never reach moral perfection, our sexual lives can be congruent with our spiritual lives, characterized by mercy, forgiveness, sin and restoration, love, joy, peace, patience, and self-control.

Heterosexuality is a concept that is barely a hundred years old, and its meaning has changed even in that brief time. Today it is a concept that breeds hierarchy, moral superiority and inauthenticity, and is not a good enough value to prize, seek after and organize life around. Thus, the end of sexual identity is the beginning of discernment.

From cure to care. Religion writer Thomas Moore asserts about
soul care, "A major difference between care and cure is that cure
implies the end of trouble. If you are cured, you don't have to worry
about whatever was bothering you any longer. But care has a sense
of ongoing attention. There is no end."[10] His wisdom applies to
sexuality as well. We may wish for quick cures for sexual problems, but often, results are neither quick nor definitive. Studies
such as Yarhouse and Jones's are sometimes used by critics to de-
nounce ex-gay ministries and therapies. The criticism is deserved
when Christians guarantee victory over misdirected sexual desire.
Increasingly, however, Christians are honestly and thoughtfully
assessing these interventions, promoting a quality of care that
should characterize all Christian communities.

Anthropologist Tanya Erzen spent eighteen months researching
New Hope Ministries, an ex-gay residential program for men
founded by Frank and Anita Worthen in San Rafael, California.[11]
"Ex-gay," in her estimate, was more of a religious identity than a
sexual one; most men did not become straight or even experience
significant change in their sexual feelings. In her book, however,
she relays perspective from Bob Davies, the former North American director of Exodus International, an umbrella organization for
Christian homosexual healing ministries: "We know behind
closed doors that change is possible, but change is rarely complete.
I know many men who are totally transformed compared to twenty
years ago, but that doesn't mean that they never have a thought or
a memory or a temptation or a struggle. It means that the struggle
has diminished significantly. It means that for all of us, redemption is still incomplete."[12]

Despite ongoing same-sex attraction and an absence of opposite-sex attraction, Jeanette Howard is committed to living as a
celibate woman. In response to pressure to become heterosexual,
or at least to deny her homosexual feelings, she tried for years to
suppress her sexuality altogether. Now she uses 2 Corinthians

12:9-10 to interpret her same-sex feelings as a weakness through which Christ's power may be displayed: "Therefore I will boast all the more gladly about my weaknesses, so that Christ's power may rest on me. That is why, for Christ's sake, I delight in weaknesses, in insults, in hardships, in persecutions, in difficulties. For when I am weak, then I am strong." Demanding nothing from God, not even resolution of her same-sex feelings, she invites others with same-sex desire to "offer it as part of your living sacrifice."[13]

When homosexuality is seen as a disease to be cured, homosexuals seem like a distinct kind of (sick) people. However, when the focus is on care instead of cure, sexuality can be acknowledged for what it really is: a valuable part of human life in which we embody conflicted desires, and through which we receive grace. All humans are beloved children of God, each with a unique sexual story, and all of us are invited to understand ourselves, make meaning of our sexual feelings and behaviors, and grow toward greater congruence between what we value and how we live.

They Are Us

Toward the end of the semester Gregory wrote a personal essay titled "God as Drag." In it, he talked about a night when he was at a bar where a dancing drag queen caught his eye. To the rhythm of loud techno music, the dancer moved in and out of the pulsing light, and seemed to move in and out of genders—man one moment, woman the next. In an instant, Gregory was filled with love. Isn't God like a drag queen, he wrote, full of mystery and beauty, never entirely what we expect or imagine, moving in and out of our lives with grace? He was the only person in class to have such an insight. Without him, we wouldn't have considered how God's grace can burst into our lives in unexpected ways, and we wouldn't have gotten to hear his story about how he was fitting together his sexuality and his spirituality.

Christian communities can't afford to play out cultural scripts, honoring heterosexuals and maligning homosexuals, seating the supposedly sexually pure at the table and leaving the sinners out in the cold. Bob Davies said it well: for all of us, redemption is incomplete. We need to set a place at the table for people with conflicted desires, inconsistent behavior and complicated sexual journeys. And if we really receive them, we'll realize that *they* are *us*.

6

Having Sex Is
(Not) a Big Deal

When James and I were engaged, we read a Christian book about marriage. The author described sex as mind-blowing, spirit-renewing and soul-altering, claiming that sex would bring intimacy and pleasure beyond what we could even dream. It would touch on the divine, renewing worship and prayer. And it could only be described with metaphors such as mountaintops, sunlight and wind. About a decade later, James picked that book up again and read a few pages aloud. We laughed at how those ethereal metaphors are still incomprehensible, and how the book promised far more than marriage can deliver. What would the author think now? we wondered, since, when he wrote the book, he was a virgin engaged to be married. He was encouraging his readers to ponder the heights and depths of something that he too was trying to imagine.

Several months after our wedding, after imagination had turned to reality, James said to me, "It's kind of disappointing how marriage isn't magically turning me into a better person." The modern Western romantic ideal of true love promises instant transformation of dust into gold when true lovers meet. The accompanying ideal of sexual fulfillment promises indescribable erotic ecstasy. All too often, instead of correcting these false promises, Christianity lays a blessing over them, offering Christian marriage as the quick ticket to true love and great sex.

The sexual identity framework distorts expectations for sex to the detriment of both married and unmarried people. But we can cultivate a realistic and redemptive view of sex. In fact, I believe that, if given attention and care, sexual activity—inside or outside of marriage—can inspire repentance and renewal.

Having Sex Is Not a Big Deal

In a *Christianity Today* article, "The Truth About Sex," I critiqued Christian absorption of cultural myths about sex being easy, fun and free.[1] Even within Christian marriage, I wrote, sex is like everything else in life: sometimes easy and sometimes difficult, sometimes fun and sometimes not, and it never comes for free. Some readers complained that the article was depressing. A measure of their hopes for marriage and their motivation for premarital chastity hinged on the promise of great sex in marriage.

My intent was not to rain on anyone's parade but to encourage realism. Sexual feelings are important, but when they're taken for more than they really are (to establish human identity) they disappoint. What is true of sexual feelings is also true of sex. It is important and good, but it can't be taken for more than what it is. Sex may be meaningful, intimate, procreative and even sacred; in these ways, it is a big deal. But when sex is expected to deliver self-actualization and consistently out-of-this-world physical pleasure, it tends to disappoint.

The idol of sexual fulfillment has two faces: One face says that each person has the right to be sexually satisfied and that having sex is a necessary part of happy, mature adulthood (or even adolescence). The second face is a Christian one that says the reward for premarital sexual virtue is great marital sex. When I was growing up, sexual ethics was all stick and no carrot: we were told to abstain from premarital sex because of the parental and divine punishment that would ensue. Today the stick is still there, but there's also a carrot: the less you sin before marriage, the hotter the sex after marriage.

Making sexual fulfillment an idol overinflates the meaning of sex with myths that are potentially damaging to everyone, sexually active or not. One myth is that sexual fulfillment is possible. Dictionary definitions of the word *fulfill* include "to make full" or "to develop the full potentialities of" or "to bring to completion." In this sense, *fulfill* is synonymous with achieving, concluding, finishing and hitting the bull's-eye. But how could a person even know whether she or he is experiencing the full potential of sexual pleasure?

By its very definition, sexual fulfillment is comparative. In high school, I remember wondering whether I had fallen in love, and I compared feelings, love notes and juicy details with my friends. In college, women compared details of romantic feelings, trying to discern whether their love was sufficient for engagement, or whether a relationship leading to marriage ought to have something more. After marriage, comparisons continue. Magazine polls provide points of reference for sexual frequency or satisfaction. Movie scripts set a standard for the romance of real-world courtships and marriages. We wonder if what we have is the real deal, or whether there might be something more.

It seems, then, that pursuing fulfillment is the least likely way to capture it. Whether it's the perfect pair of pants, a dream house or a great sex life, measuring what we have against the standard of imagined total satisfaction mires us in dissatisfaction, leaving us comparing ourselves to others and worrying that we might be missing the good life. Instead of living more deeply into what we already have, we're encouraged to believe fulfillment is just a purchase, relationship or experience away.

Another myth is that Christian marriage guarantees great sex. In marked contrast to the unmarried readers who were disappointed by my "Truth About Sex" article, some married readers resonated with my thesis, sharing stories of difficult marriages and troubled sex lives made worse by Christian pressure to smile and pretend everything is fine. There are many reasons why, even in a good marriage, sex is less than mind-blowingly, soul-alteringly, life-fulfillingly awesome in every instance. It can be negatively affected by health conditions, medications, pornography use or addiction, stress or unhappiness, fertility, infertility, past or present trauma, or differences between spouses about what constitutes enjoyable sex. What's more, for better and for worse, sex changes over time in a marriage as people age and experience different seasons of life.

But even if a marriage lacks great sex for a while—even for a long while—it can still exhibit sexual holiness. Take, for instance, a marriage in which one person is healing from past sexual trauma, or is assaulted after marriage in a way that impacts his or her sexuality. This may influence the frequency and quality of sexual intercourse, but the love expressed in the relationship may be healing and restorative. Or consider a couple with young children: the combination of pregnancy, nursing hormones and fatigue may have squelched the sexual energy of the wife, the husband or both. Neither spouse may be sexually fulfilled for an entire season of the marriage, but love is abounding.

Don't get me wrong: a marriage in which sex is mutually enjoyable and abundantly available is preferable to one in which sex is painful, unwanted or the source of conflict. And there certainly are sound reasons for divorce; sticking with a troubled marriage isn't always the high road. But if personal fulfillment is the standard by which sexual well-being is measured, most married people—at some time or another—would have reason to go shopping for better sex.

In one sense, then, having sex isn't such a big deal. It just isn't true that, in order to be a happy, healthy adult, a person must explore his or her sexual feelings, choose a corresponding sexual identity, and live out that identity through sexual activity. For some married Christians, absorption of these beliefs leads to disappointment when marriage can't live up to unrealistic expectations. These beliefs also sometimes compel same-sex-attracted Christians to choose marriage as a way to either force themselves to be heterosexual or portray themselves as such to others. And for those who want to be married but aren't, these beliefs can entrench the sense that, without sexual intimacy in marriage, the good life is out of reach.

Having Sex Is a Big Deal

In other ways, of course, sex is a really big deal. The first biblical story that includes sex is about Adam and Eve, and it illustrates sexual holiness well.

> Now the man knew his wife Eve, and she conceived and bore Cain, saying, "I have produced a man with the help of the Lord." Next she bore his brother Abel. (Genesis 4:1-2 NRSV)

The English word "knew" is translated from the Hebrew *yada,* which carries many nuances of meaning, several of which serve the sexual euphemism well. *Yada* means to know by experience, to perceive and discern, or to recognize.[2] It connotes a deep, personal knowing. Speaking of knowledge in general, Steve Garber makes the case that Hebrew relational epistemology could help curb the extremes of modern Western technical, objectifying knowledge.[3] When we were colleagues at the American Studies Program, he put it this way in his lectures: "To know about is to care for, is to have responsibility for." Students in that program learned the inherent connections between knowledge (specifically knowledge of politics and public life), love and responsibility. His perspective on knowledge is helpful in the area of sexuality as well.

The part of Adam and Eve's story that could have been erotic and, in a romance novel, might ramble on for pages is summed up in just five words: "the man knew his wife Eve." Most of the narrative is about family; sex brought Cain into being, and then Abel. Eve's comment, "I have produced a man with the help of the LORD," shows how sex connected her to God, her husband and her sons, all relationships of great care and responsibility. Sexual knowing is part of sexual holiness when people come to more deeply recognize, understand and take responsibility in their relationships to self, others and God.

In this light, sex, like marriage in general, is only partly about the individual and his or her desires; it is always also about others. Certainly the other partner in the marriage is important. But there is a host of absent others: it is an act of love toward all others in the world to refrain from sex with them. And there are potential others: children not yet conceived, adopted or even wanted. Many sexual relationships (though certainly not all) carry the possibility of children, even those that seem to exclude the possibility, such as same-sex relationships, relationships in which one or both partners are infertile, or relationships in which people use contraception. Over time, sexual intimacy often leads to the desire for children, whether by intercourse, assisted reproduction or adoption. In its sexual dimension, then, marriage is not primarily a dispenser of pleasure for individuals; rather, it connects the self with one other, and expresses love for all others, even those who exist only as possibilities.

Considering sex from an ancient Hebrew point of view emphasizes the importance of making more of sex. If sex is seen as just the act of intercourse, or even more narrowly, just orgasm, then it becomes a desirable commodity to get and to have. Sex is more than contact between body parts; it is contact between human beings who influence and are influenced by their communities. *Yada* is more than just having sex, or even the sum total of all the acts of sexual intercourse in a relationship over time. It's all of the knowing, perceiving, discerning and familiarity accumulated over time in a relationship that includes sex as just one part of life shared between two people. Physical sexual knowledge is part of a greater whole—a marriage that, at best, is like any other Christian practice characterized by love, grace, repentance and so on. If marriage or marital sex is asked to deliver self-actualization or good sex on tap, it is likely to disappoint. But it can excel at what it is designed for: drawing people more and more deeply toward love.

Practicing sex, over and over in the course of a marriage, makes plain that sexual intimacy is not an opportunity to get, have, or do a person or an experience. Instead, it is an opportunity to give and receive love, joy, peace, patience, kindness, goodness, faithfulness, gentleness and self-control (Galatians 5:22-23). The fruit of the Spirit ripens in the body.

Marriage as a Crucible

A friend, contemplating divorce and looking for affirmation, asked me whether I frequently consider leaving my husband. I said, "I'm sympathetic to your struggle, but no, I don't daydream about the single life I could be living. Most of the time I enjoy my marriage, but there are low points too. When happiness seems like a distant possibility, I tell myself, 'Marriage is my crucible.'"

In a laboratory, a crucible is a container that's made of material strong enough to hold very hot or acidic chemical reactions. Marriage may be seen as a crucible for all that happens sexually between two people, and sexual satisfaction is only one of those things. Sexuality is all about reactions—whether in behavior, thoughts or feelings—that can be heated, volatile or unexpected. Good sex arouses the body, to be sure, but it also awakens emotion, hope and memory. Sexual holiness includes receiving and caring for all that sex arouses in both people over time. For most couples, this demonstrates the paradox of suffering and blessing being simultaneously present in the life of holiness.

The sexual identity framework encourages us to focus on inner sexual feelings and then use them to define our identities and as a venue for pursuing self-fulfillment. Though heterosexual married Christians may seem to be the moral victors when this framework is applied, it can be damaging for them too when it offers distorted expectations for marriage. Theologian Mildred Wynkoop writes that as a person matures in holiness, she or he finds Christ at the center of love.[4] Applying her point to sex means that the center of sexual love is neither orgasm (as the pinnacle of fulfillment) nor sexual feelings (as the center of personal identity). Holiness in sexuality is the same as holiness in any part of life; it's the life of love, centered in Christ.

Seeking personal sexual satisfaction is a legitimate part of sexual holiness in marriage. Sex feels good, and if and when it doesn't, it's well worth trying to improve it. And marriage may be a source of intense sexual gratification and happiness, which is wonderful. But it may also be the context within which people encounter and learn to accept sexual limitations and disappointments. If Christian marriage is viewed as the reward for premarital chastity, the disappointments may be unnecessarily exaggerated. Viewing marriage as a crucible highlights the strength, shelter and resilience that marriage can offer, even for the complexities of sexuality.

Sex Outside the Crucible

In the Sermon on the Mount, Jesus heightened the already rigorous sexual standards of Hebrew law. He explained that adultery is not just a matter of physical sexual contact; in fact, any man who looks at a woman with lust in his heart has already committed adultery with her, and such a man should tear his eye out to avoid being thrown into hell (Matthew 5:27-30).

Jesus practiced this teaching in an unexpected way, however. In the temple one day he encountered a woman who was forced to stand before Jewish religious leaders while they asked Jesus whether or not to stone her (John 8:1-11). (They were likely more concerned with trying to elicit a response that would diminish Jesus' reputation, but still, Jesus' response to adultery is very important.) Based on the Sermon on the Mount, I might expect Jesus to escalate the punishment just as he had escalated the meaning of the violation. Perhaps he would tear the woman's eye out and tell her it was a mercy that would save her from hell. Perhaps he would do the same to the man with whom she sinned. Jesus did not make a quick judgment, though. In fact, he seemed to do nothing; he simply bent down and wrote in the sand with his finger. When he stood again, he permitted the stoning, but with this caveat: only a person without sin could throw the first stone. Writing in the sand again while everyone walked away, Jesus then told the woman that he did not condemn her. "Go your way, and from now on do not sin again," he said (John 8:11 NRSV).

Biblical scholar Michael Cosby synthesizes the apparent contradiction between Jesus' words and actions: "Jesus' statements pertaining to sexuality reveal an amazing combination of forceful demands for complete purity and gentle treatment of those who were guilty of sexual offenses."[5] Jesus models what it means to have a renewed mind, able to discern what is good, perfect and pleasing. Maybe when he bent down to write in the sand, he was pausing to consider the situation. His posture of careful consideration would have contrasted sharply with that of the religious leaders who stood confidently, measuring out a punishment. Maybe he discerned that more than one sin had been committed. The sin of adultery was important, but by the standard of looking at a woman with lust, all the men had sinned too. The sin of haughtiness was also evident, and was being neglected entirely. Jesus called everyone to repentance. Both the religious leaders and the woman were invited to rethink their behaviors, and were given the opportunity to walk away changed.

In their haughtiness (and in the adultery they likely committed by looking at women lustfully), the men judging the adulterous woman had committed the same sin as her: failing to keep the law. Paul rails against religious leaders who pass judgment on others while committing the same sins themselves: "Do you imagine, whoever you are, that when you judge those who do such things and yet do them yourself, you will escape the judgment of God? Or do you despise the riches of his kindness and forbearance and patience? Do you not realize that God's kindness is meant to lead you to repentance?" (Romans 2:3-4 NRSV). These teachings ring painfully true with respect to sexuality in the church today. Male pastors preach against homosexuality but secretly have sex with men themselves. Church leaders decry sexual immorality but view Internet pornography in their offices. Advocates for the sanctity of marriage have affairs. Phoniness like this caused Paul to quote Isaiah's lament, "The name of God is blasphemed among the Gentiles" (Romans 2:24 NRSV). In our day, Christians and non-Christians alike despise religious institutions that harbor hypocrisy.

In a church I attended, Pastor Wayne sexually abused boys. People had complained for years, but nothing was done. Eventually, a legal complaint landed Pastor Wayne in prison. A teenager at the time, I was horrified to see church leaders refuse to share relevant details with the congregation and move on as if the problem had been successfully swept away. Pastor Wayne had problems, to be sure, but so did all of us who participated in his ministry. Some people had complained about being abused and were ignored or even maligned. Some of us kids had friends who were abused, and we didn't know what to do with our memories of their stories. Some adults had actively protected Pastor Wayne by ignoring complaints, pushing abused children and their families out of the church, propping up Pastor Wayne's reputation, and ensuring his ongoing access to private time with children. We all needed to repent, to rethink how our church and denomination might better protect children, identify and care for sexually demented adults, and handle the power and responsibility that flow through church structures. In this case, the church offered a false forbearance and patience, one that allowed a man's sin to flourish.

Later, I visited another church and was surprised when someone told me Pastor Joe was sitting in the congregation each week while the youth pastor led weekly services. Turns out Pastor Joe had recently had an affair. When he was found out, he put himself at the mercy of the church leadership board, offering to resign or do whatever seemed best. The board asked him to disclose his sin to the congregation, undergo counseling and remain in the church as an active member of the congregation. Leaders stayed in close contact with Pastor Joe; after months passed they assessed his situation and asked him to step back up to his pastoral responsibilities with a new accountability process in place. When he began preaching again, Pastor Joe talked about his sin very frankly and shared what he had learned about self-righteousness, denial, restoration, and healthy sexuality and marriage. It was a painful process, especially for his family, but the church board's kindness led the congregation to repentance. Pastor Joe repented, or thought anew, about his roles in church and family, and his personal spiritual journey. Congregants thought anew about sin and redemption in their own lives, prompted by the real-life journey of holiness being played out in front of them.

Comparing these three situations—the woman caught in adultery, a pedophile pastor and a male religious leader caught in adultery—is like comparing apples and oranges, and that's precisely the point. There is no single approach that would suit these three situations, not to mention myriad other examples. A same-sex-attracted man pursues anonymous sex in public places. An engaged Christian couple decides to begin having sex shortly before marriage. A woman has an emotional affair that, while not physical, breaks her commitment to love and honor her husband. A teenager loses his virginity with someone he hardly knows, just so he can tell his friends. A same-sex couple adopts and raises a family. Instances of sex outside the crucible of marriage abound.

It would be foolish to tear Pastor Joe's eyes out when he was willing to submit to a process of restoration. (It would also be foolish to misunderstand Jesus' hyperbole as plain speech.) It would be foolish to tell Pastor Wayne, "Go on your way and sin no more," because he had committed crimes and was likely to continue doing so. Jesus' response to the woman caught in adultery teaches us to fully understand a situation before acting—to pause, bend down and write with a finger in the sand—and then respond with the kindness and forbearance that inspires repentance. (One note: in Pastor Wayne's case, public exposure and imprisonment was a kindness; he eventually acknowledged the harm he had done and accepted permanent and profound accountability measures.)

Go on Your Way

Both heterosexuality and marriage are points of privilege in the church that take people off the hook, morally speaking. The view seems to be that heterosexuals and married people may sin occasionally, but they are not sinful in their very being as homosexuals are. For many Christians, homosexuality pads the bottom of the sin barrel, so no matter how low a heterosexual may go, at least she or he hasn't gone as low as *them*. In addition, by privileging heterosexuality over homosexuality, Christian appropriations of sexual identity categories tend to make heterosexual marriage the end instead of Christlikeness.

Living in accordance with Romans 12:1-2 by perceiving our culture's sexual identity categories and being transformed so we no longer live under their spell reduces both heterosexual privilege and homosexual subjugation. When heterosexual persons, and heterosexual married persons even more, stop thinking of ourselves more highly than we ought, we'll find ourselves in conversation with those we once might have considered targets for outreach. Sexual identity categories distract us from the calling that rings true for everyone: "You are not condemned. Go on your way, and do not sin again."

7

Celibacy Is
(Not) a Big Deal

Celibacy has never been wildly popular, but these days its reputation may be sinking even further. A Christian father mentioned to me the commitment his daughter and her fiancé made to remain chaste until marriage. The parent smiled quizzically and commented, "It's kind of quaint, but if that's what they believe, then I'm sure it will be good for them." A friend of mine, committed to celibacy until her late twenties, started having sex with a casual boyfriend. She justified her decision with anger, saying, "I did my part—remained a virgin—and God didn't give me a Christian husband. I'm done waiting." A young Christian woman learning about homosexuality through the experience of her best friend, a gay man, wondered, "Why would God want homosexuals to be celibate, when a straight person at least has the chance at a fulfilled life?"

Other Christians believe very strongly in the importance of preserving sexual intimacy for marriage between a man and a woman, but even then it can be hard to stick to. Teenagers take vows before God, their peers and their parents to remain chaste until marriage, but still, most have premarital sex, though at later ages than their peers.[1] Christians with same-sex attractions pursue reparative therapy, attempting to change their sexual feelings or to remain chaste, but many are unable to do so.[2] As more Christian adults remain unmarried, or marry later, many find it difficult to practice or even discuss celibacy as it was taught to them in youth group.[3]

Even those who strongly affirm marriage as an exclusive context for sex may wince at the prospect of lifelong celibacy. Whether it's before marriage for young adults, long-term for singles, potentially lifelong for partners in a sexless marriage or permanent for Christians with same-sex attraction, celibacy may seem implausible, old-fashioned, and even unhealthy or dangerous, even in the eyes of committed Christians. A God who would deny sexual happiness to entire classes of people based on criteria beyond their control may seem mean, not gracious. And a religion that requires people to refrain from mutually pleasurable intimacy that doesn't seem to hurt anyone may seem capricious. In a society that idolizes sexual fulfillment, permanent celibacy doesn't seem like the easy yoke and light burden Jesus promised (Matthew 11:30). People are more likely to invoke other sayings of Jesus—with a gulp, perhaps—such as Luke 1:37 (NIV): "For nothing is impossible with God."

I'm still convinced that celibacy is an honorable way of life for faithful Christians, but at the same time I see reason upon reason why it is falling out of favor and out of practice. Just as is true for sex in marriage, the support structures for celibacy need strengthening. Irrespective of the integrity or maturity of the person practicing it, celibacy carries opposite potentials: it can be a burden that results in depression and personal harm, or a spiritual practice that brings intimacy and human flourishing.

Celibacy as Nonsense

Whether it's in the area of shopping, sports, jobs or sex, Western values encourage people to discover what they really want and then go for it; the happy person is one who can freely do what he or she wants to do. Desire and action are closely linked, so harmony between wanting and doing is believed to bring fulfillment. I remember a conversation between me, a secular friend (Susan) and a Christian friend (Lisa) who was engaged and committed to abstaining from sex until marriage. Susan was concerned about the absence of sex in Lisa's relationship. She said, "You won't know whether or not you're sexually compatible until after marriage, and then there's too much at stake. You're marrying someone you don't really know." Lisa explained her belief that sexual compatibility is based on more than the act of sex, and that strong communication, a desire for sex with each other (which she and her fiancé had in abundance) and their commitment to each other all predict an ability to make a sexual relationship work. Then Susan said, "I don't want to be too invasive here, but I just worry that you don't really want to have sex with him. If you really felt sexual longing, you'd be having sex. If you're not doing it, it must be because you don't really want to." In this view, chastity seems like a dangerous delusion, not a moral benefit. (Lisa's report after the honeymoon was very positive, and years later, their marriage is solid.)

Our pursuit of happiness is not without limits, of course. The principle of harm guides many U.S. legal prohibitions against sexual contact. For example, adults are forbidden from pursuing sexual contact with minors (regardless of the desires of either party), and with any nonconsenting adult. But in the U.S. and in other Western nations, both the law and cultural norms permit sex before marriage and without marriage, between consenting adults. The system leans toward freedom, restraining one person only when necessary to preserve another's rights or well-being.

When biblical teachings prohibit behaviors that don't seem to directly harm the participants, it can be difficult for people living under a harm-based legal system to understand or value these teachings. People in areas such as Asia and the Arab world may understand the original context of these teachings more readily because they perceive individual actions as influencing family shame and honor. Indeed, biblical scholar Donald Wold argues that while Old Testament law does address interpersonal harm, it doesn't lean so heavily on the principle of harm for justifying sexual prohibitions. In Wold's view, Old Testament laws are based on a variety of values including interpersonal harm, consideration of the entire community, care for potential offspring and the character of God.[4]

Besides our harm-based legal system, another influence that makes celibacy seem implausible is increased exposure to sexuality in media. In addition to images that are destructive and distorted, we see love and sexual intimacy between people who are married and not married, and between people of the opposite sex and the same sex. Growing up in the 1980s, I never saw a gay character in a TV show or movie and rarely saw any sexual scenes; for most of my childhood we didn't have cable TV, a computer or a VCR. Sexual images were only available to adults who could purchase magazines or movie admittance or who sought out other points of access outside the home. As a young adult, I vividly remember seeing the movie *Philadelphia*, in which a gay man is fired from his job when his colleagues discover he has AIDS. I had never seen a gay relationship either in the real world or in a movie. *Philadelphia* raised the possibility that gay people may be caring, sympathetic, decent human beings, and that their relationships may be loving and deeply committed. Media exposure and, later, friendships with real people, showed me that my Christian ethics weren't based only in Scripture, as I would have claimed—they were also based in ignorance of and abhorrence toward people whose sexual practices weren't "Christian."

In all these ways, celibacy is rendered nonsense in the literal definition of the word: nonsense is a communication that does not carry meaning in a particular context. From the perspective of dominant cultural values, it's difficult to understand the logic of sexual holiness: That desire warrants discipline and care, not fulfillment and affirmation. That celibacy can nurture human flourishing, but even when it doesn't, it's still an honorable choice. That, for a Christian, the pool of potential sexual partners is very, very small: either one (a spouse) or zero.

Obviously, humans can live without sex; having sex is a choice, and anyone can choose to not do it. But all too often, Christian discussions of sexual ethics stop there, with airtight pronouncements about the moral fortitude each individual should have, irrespective of the relational or cultural context. Sexual decision making is not entirely personal, however. Choices are often made in relationship with a lover or potential lover, and, as we've seen, that relationship has a cultural context that shapes how people think about and talk about sex. Western beliefs about desire and freedom, new media, and other factors encourage us to be more generous about whether, and with whom, we pursue sexual pleasure. The Christian religion lauds celibacy for the unmarried, but as I'll argue later, Christian support for celibacy is often not strong enough on a practical level to counterbalance the broader cultural dismissal of it.

A Different Sense

It's not only important that Christianity is true; it must also be plausible. A plausibility structure is the cultural framework—the language, beliefs, assumptions and norms—that supports a way of life.[5] It's a concept that describes how a group of people come to share a sense of what is believable, or plausible. In large-scale societies, many plausibility structures are at play simultaneously, which means individuals are enculturated into some but are also able to choose some.

Sexual holiness is strange, and celibacy all the more, because they aren't reinforced by dominant plausibility structures. Those of us pursuing sexual holiness can relate to what the author of Hebrews writes after listing many heroes of the faith: "All these people were still living by faith when they died. They did not receive the things promised; they only saw them and welcomed them from a distance. And they admitted that they were aliens and strangers on earth. People who say such things show that they are looking for a country of their own" (Hebrews 11:13-14 NIV). Whether married, single and hoping to be married, single and satisfied, living with some degree of same-sex desire, or some combination of these, the practice of holiness makes strangers and aliens of us all.

In studying celibacy in crosscultural perspective, anthropologists have found it does not have the same meaning everywhere. In some cultures, celibacy may be a sign that a person is flawed or odd; in others it may signify spiritual commitment, enlightenment or exceptional self-control.[6] For example, in Hinduism, *brahmacharya* refers to a phase of life in which celibacy is seen as extremely important for spiritual development; it may also refer to a permanent vow of spirituality that includes restricted sexuality. Shaker Christians renounce sex altogether for spiritual reasons, vowing to abstain from any desire-inducing behaviors such as kissing, and reproduction as well. (Shakers are few in number, but they are still an active Christian tradition.) For Catholics, the time-honored monastic vocation provides a social role and a shared way of life for celibates.

Long-term celibacy becomes plausible when there are widely held values, positive language, meaningful social roles and real social support for celibates. For example, a church could review the language used to describe its groups and programs, and make sure they make room for celibates (Sunday school classes labeled "young marrieds" or "empty nesters" imply that being married with children is the norm). A Christian organization could ensure that its health-care benefits and sick/medical-leave provisions don't unfairly privilege married people with children. In a group of friends in which only a few are celibate, language and practices that respect everyone equally could be cultivated (avoiding the common assumption that celibate people must have lots of spare time for volunteering, for instance, or that their commitments aren't as serious as parents' commitments). Married people could acknowledge the family experience and personal insights of celibate people by discussing the struggles of sexuality, pregnancy or parenting with them.

Celibacy should be an invitation, not a punishment. In order for it to be an invitation worth responding to, however, Christian communities must cultivate plausibility structures for sexual holiness in which long-term celibacy becomes not just moral, but also plausible and practical. When they practice it and support it, Christians keep the possibility (and the plausibility) of celibacy alive, both for our own communities and for the surrounding society.

The Unchaste Church

In a church workshop on homosexuality, I led a learning activity in which I wrote "I want you!" on poster board and invited participants to list what people want when they say they "want" another person in a sexual way. The list went on and on; sexual relationships are desirable because they offer friendship, companionship, love, touch, marriage, intimacy, financial stability, old-age security, children, pregnancy, social respectability, health insurance and, of course, sexual pleasure. Having sex is about so much more than just having sex.

For Christians who value sexual holiness, marriage seems to be the key that unlocks the door to all these good things. Without marriage, a person may well miss out on loving touch, life in a household, positive contact with children, companionship, financial stability, health insurance, and certainty of care when he or she is sick or aging. Moreover, without marriage, Christians may be marooned in the "young adult" group at their church, no matter their age, and never fit with the "life stage" categories of Sunday school classes and small groups. They may be asked to volunteer or give more than others under the assumption that they have lots of free time. And to top it off, a person may have suspicions cast against them as to why they remain single. Too often, not only do churches not support celibates in positive ways, but church programs, values, language and institutional cultures often aggressively (if unintentionally) undermine them. Chastity is as much a practice as a value; while they uphold sexual purity as a value, churches are often unchaste in their practice.

A woman at the church workshop complained to me afterward, "Just because I have same-sex desire, I have to go without all of those things!" Celibacy is surely a strenuous spiritual path, but today the cost of celibacy is unreasonably and unnecessarily high. When it comes to moral teachings about sex outside of marriage, we isolate sexual pleasure from all the other good things that are connected to sexual relationships. People are commanded to abstain from sexual pleasure and intimacy, but no one addresses how abstention may also limit the person's access to family, touch, children, financial stability and so on. It's hard to be a celibate person in an unchaste church whose broader context is an unchaste society. In striving for moral virtue, the celibate also bears the church's collective sin of failing, in a highly sexualized social context, to make a counterculture in which celibacy is plausible.

Celibacy Gone Wrong

It shouldn't be surprising that, with such an unsupportive context, celibacy can actually be very damaging. Sociologist Denise Donnelly and her research team interviewed people who were involuntarily celibate.[7] Some had never had sex, others had had past relationships but were currently not in a relationship, and others were in sexless relationships. These people weren't choosing celibacy for religious reasons; sex just wasn't happening for them. Virgins described themselves as "off time," as though opportunities had passed them by and they were stalled in an earlier life stage. One woman said, "It makes me feel like everyone else is going through some mythical gates into 'grownup land' while I sit out in the courtyard with the children." Those who had had sex in the past but were either currently unpartnered or in a sexless relationship described problems with loneliness, depression, poor body image and hopelessness. A married woman in a sexless relationship described her life as "[lots of] hurt, tears. Knowing it will always be this way and missing intimacy. Forever." For many of these people, celibacy led to depression, loneliness and regret.

Even when celibacy is an intentional choice made for religious reasons, it can cause damage. For example, though Catholic priests and nuns have a strong social support system for celibacy—orders that provide purposeful service, venues for relationship and daily life in community, as well as a religious tradition that has honored celibacy for hundreds of years—psychologist Anne Hoenkamp-Bisschop's interviews with Catholic priests revealed that only some thrive.[8] Indeed, some of the priests in the study, despite efforts to comply with the rule of celibacy, couldn't meet it perfectly. About half of those she interviewed had occasional sexual relationships that were disappointing to their own moral intentions. They described less satisfaction in other relationships as well, explaining that so much energy is invested in struggling with celibacy that little is left for enjoyment of other relationships (with family members, parishioners and even God). Still others remained priests but had rejected the rule of celibacy, choosing instead long-term, exclusive sexual relationships that didn't include living together. Hoenkamp-Bisschops argues that many priests commit to celibacy as a high-minded religious ideal when they're young, and that it is only after their vows that the reality sets in. Some are able to develop satisfying friendships and other relationships, but for many others, going without sex also means going without intimacy.

Christians choose celibacy for many reasons: because they aren't married, because they believe it would be sinful to act on their same-sex attractions, because they don't see divorce or adultery as a solution to sexlessness in marriage, and others. But in the

absence of kin, church and cultural supports that would offer connections for a vibrant, stable life, Christians who choose celibacy
are often on their own to follow a difficult moral teaching. Little
wonder, then, that religious motivation doesn't resolve the problems reported by nonreligious involuntary celibates such as feeling
"off time," lonely, unloved, depressed, ugly and so on. In fact,
thriving celibates seem to be people for whom celibacy simply harmonizes with their personal makeup. The religious rule requiring
celibacy is not the main motivator for them; it is, rather, just a personal choice.

Self-Actualized Celibates

Theologian Dayna Olson-Getty says that when chosen for right
reasons and practiced in a supportive community, celibacy can be
a prophetic discipline. Like other intentional, countercultural
practices such as living simply, celibacy challenges cultural beliefs
about personal worth, identity, success and even health, and it can
cause others in the church and society to reconsider their idolatry
of romance and sex. It can also be a spiritual calling that chooses
one good (the way of Jesus) over another good (genital sexual expression). Olson-Getty summarizes, "To say 'no' to something as
powerfully magnetic as sex requires something even more powerful to which one is saying 'yes.'"[9]

One powerful benefit celibacy can yield is hospitality—an openness to and enjoyment of relationship that is enhanced by the absence of an exclusive sexual relationship. Psychologist Gerdenio
Manuel interviewed Catholic priests who said celibacy, over time,
resulted in increased depth and breadth in interpersonal relationships.[10] The absence of an exclusive sexual relationship gave them
freedom to love all people equally. After studying and worshiping
at a monastery, Kathleen Norris found this to be the case as well,
writing, "I have been told by monks and nuns that hospitality is
the fruit of their celibacy; they do not mean to scorn the flesh but

live in such a way as to remain unencumbered by exclusive, sexual relationships. The goal is being free to love others, non-exclusively and non-possessively, both within their monastic community and without."[11]

Instead of linking sexual intimacy to the long list of "wants" described at my workshop, celibates may cultivate new ways of life that can be insightful for everyone. Olson-Getty describes how "self-actualized" celibates distinguished between genital desire and psychological/emotional needs; they then pursued intimacy and personal growth through committed friendships and secured stability in finances, health care and domestic life through their religious order. This way of life, she observed, comes back around to enhance even that which was denied: "Self-actualizers are not only unharmed by celibacy, they are characterized by an unusual freedom from the sexual compulsions that often stem from repression."[12] They understood their sexual lifestyle as stemming from an intentional choice—a pursuit of a self-enriching and world-blessing purpose that necessarily excludes sexual freedom.

The Deal with Celibacy

In one sense, then, celibacy is a big deal. It can really do damage, or it can be a profound blessing. It's important to keep the possibility of celibacy alive in the church and in society by practicing it, even at great personal cost. And it's essential for all Christians to work toward cultivating communities in which sexual holiness for unmarried people is both plausible and practical.

In another sense, however, celibacy is not a big deal—or, to put it more precisely, not the biggest deal. When sexual morality becomes an idol, it dominates the landscape, prioritizing the choice for or against sexual intimacy as the choice that matters most; the options become diametrically opposed: be holy or a whore, choose God or pleasure, be a disciple or a hedonist. When people make sexual decisions, however, the choice is rarely (if ever) so stark.

It's one thing to abstain from sex for religious reasons during dating or engagement; the person who does so is also pursuing intimacy, companionship, and a future of marriage and possibly parenting. The short-term choice against sex actually increases the likelihood of having more sex later. It's another thing, however, for a persistently same-sex-attracted Christian in his thirties or forties to choose against sexual intimacy. In this case, saying no to sex means also saying no to partnership, intimacy, and all the other social and economic benefits of long-term sexual partnerships and/or marriage. There are more values at play—good values such as love, intimacy, companionship and so on—than just the value of chastity.

It's important—and, within many churches, certainly countercultural—to understand why Christians often choose against chastity. It's not always that they're choosing a bad thing (sexual hedonism) over a good thing (morality). Sometimes they might be choosing a good thing that is real (a sexual relationship outside of marriage) over a good thing that doesn't even exist (a well-supported and relationally rich celibate life in the church). Or, if they already feel judged to hell because of their sexual orientation or their sexual past, they might just be giving up on trying to meet the impossible standards set by other Christians.

Martin Luther wrote, "Be a sinner, and let your sins be strong, but let your trust in Christ be stronger, and rejoice in Christ who is the victor over sin, death, and the world." He followed this bold assertion with a sexual example: "No sin can separate us from Him, even if we were to kill or commit adultery thousands of times each day. Do you think such an exalted Lamb paid merely a small price with a meager sacrifice for our sins? Pray hard, for you are quite a sinner."[13] When Christians, or the institutional cultures of local churches, regulate people's sexual behavior by using shame or gossip, or by using access to resources as "sticks" and insider status, love and affirmation as "carrots," we encourage people toward right behavior for wrong reasons. It would be better to sin and experience the immensity of grace than to avoid sin for fear of disapproval, banishment, or loss of employment or leadership roles in the church. When we allow sin to become the criterion by which people are labeled, divided and judged, we are actually proclaiming sin to be the victor over people, not showing how Christ is the victor over sin. Somewhat similar to Luther on this point, John Wesley's view of holiness suggests that God's love is always available to us, and that we are always able to reach out to God and to our neighbors. Our identities are permanently altered by love and grace, not by sexual sin or sexual virtue.

A Particular Gift

As a (reasonably happily) married woman, I hesitate to describe the benefits or drawbacks of celibacy. I don't know the struggles or the blessings from firsthand experience, but I believe Christian married people and celibates share this in common: religious pressure to be (or at least look) happy and blessed as a sign of God's favor. Whether it's the joy of marriage or parenting or the spiritual enlightenment of celibacy, Christians often feel as though the responsibility of self-actualization is pinned on them. Like sex itself, Jesus becomes a consumer good; we market him like a car or shampoo: "Just buy this, and the good life is yours." A difficult marriage, challenging parenting or unhappy celibacy is beneficial for exposing this marketing strategy; the truth is that "buying" Jesus doesn't make life easy or perfect. The ease of one's celibacy (or marriage) is not necessarily an indicator of the quality of one's faith. Sexual struggle, whether in celibacy or marriage or nonmarital relationships, is not a problem to be stuffed away. If it's well cared for, sexual disappointment can become like the apostle Paul's "thorn"—an enduring hardship that inspires a reliance on grace (2 Corinthians 12:1-10).

Of course, while we don't know exactly what Paul's thorn was, we know it wasn't celibacy in and of itself. He wished that more Christian men could live as he did, free from the duties associated with being a husband and father. Paul seemed to relish the ability he had to invest all his time and energy in promoting Jesus' message and building up churches. For some, like him, celibacy is considered "a particular gift from God" (1 Corinthians 7:7 NRSV). For others, celibacy can, over time, become a way of life that brings love, joy and abundance to the celibate person and their community.

Epilogue

The End Is Near

For as in one body we have many members, and not all the members have the same function, so we, who are many, are one body in Christ, and individually we are members one of another. We have gifts that differ according to the grace given to us: prophecy, in proportion to faith; ministry, in ministering; the teacher, in teaching; the exhorter, in exhortation; the giver, in generosity; the leader, in diligence; the compassionate, in cheerfulness.

Let love be genuine; hate what is evil, hold fast to what is good; love one another with mutual affection; outdo one another in showing honor.

ROMANS 12:4-10 NRSV

As the human body is, so is the body of Christ. Understanding Paul's metaphor therefore requires a healthy understanding of the human body. With a classroom learning exercise called "The Body Project," I played with the metaphor: what if we really did treat the body of Christ the way we treat our own bodies? Each of the thirty students in the class received an index card with a body part written on it: eyes, ears, face, skin, ankles, breasts, fingernails and so on. Then each student listed on his or her card every possible flaw of that part and taped the cards to the board in the shape of a body, each card in the place of its part. I read their lists aloud as quickly as I could, but it took quite a while; there were over two hundred potential flaws. Hair could be too thin, sparse, long, short, dry, oily, curly, straight or poorly styled. Arms could be too muscular, thin, long, short, pale, moley, saggy, pimply or hairy. Legs could be too long, short, fat, lumpy, scrawny, hairy or have cellulite. Even seemingly unoffending parts such as ankles or elbows weren't let off the hook (elbows could be too dry, wrinkly, fat or baggy, and ankles could be cankles).

Beauty is a good thing, but not when it inspires hundreds of rules which any individual is bound to violate. That's a common distortion of beauty in modern societies that encourage people to treat their bodies as projects. Judging thirty or more body parts against dozens of standards of perfection (many of us do this daily) cultivates a judging mind which we then use in other parts of life as well.

Sexual purity is a good thing too, but when it is reduced to law, it produces shame, repression, superiority and division. Like the body, sexuality becomes a project: we assess it, maintain it, fix it, renovate it and hide its flaws. Others' sexualities are turned into projects too when, instead of offering genuine love and mutual affection, we become the contractor they didn't ask for, sizing up their sexuality and offering a blueprint for improvement. Churches and other Christian communities such as non-profits, companies or colleges may institutionalize a project mentality by creating processes, programs and personnel structures that honor some people more than others on the basis of their spirituality, symbolized in part by their sexuality. Thus, we may often live by Paul's advice, treating each other in the church the way we treat our own bodies, but not in the way he intended. One student looked at the index-card body on the chalkboard and summed it up: "That may be a body, but it sure isn't the body of Christ."

The Unpresentable Parts

In 1 Corinthians 12, Paul develops the body metaphor in greater detail.

> Those parts of the body that seem to be weaker are indispensable, and the parts that we think are less honorable we treat with special honor. And the parts that are unpresentable are treated with special modesty, while our presentable parts need no special treatment. But God has combined the members of the body and has given greater honor to the parts that lacked it, so that there should be no division in the body, but that its parts should have equal concern for each other. (1 Corinthians 12:22-25 NIV)

It's not entirely clear what Paul meant by "the parts that are unpresentable," but it's probably safe to assume that sexual body parts would be included. Unpresentable parts may not be suitable for public display, but they are not unmentionable; special modesty does not require bashfulness or reticence. In fact, the writers of Scripture offer fresh metaphors for private body parts that renew cultural understandings in ways that give greater honor to these parts and new insight into life in general.

For Jews and Jewish followers of Christ, circumcision was a "flag" for ethnic belonging. Circumcision (or uncircumcision) marked a man and his family as insiders (or outsiders) to the Jewish way of life. Early on in Hebrew history it was a practice that united a group of people, but in the early church it did just the opposite, dividing Jewish believers from Gentile believers. Paul deflated the meaning of circumcision, reminding Jewish believers of the fullest original meaning of the practice: circumcision is valuable as an outward sign of genuine devotion to God, but the real circumcision is "spiritual and not literal," the circumcision of the heart (Romans 2:29; see also Deuteronomy 30:6). Believers were to stop using an unpresentable body part as a symbol of superior standing in the church by virtue of ethnicity. In fact, equally valuing circumcised and uncircumcised penises (and, more importantly, the men to whom they belonged) is an example of all the parts having equal concern for each other.

In biblical cultures, women's sexual parts were, in one sense, overvalued insofar as women were valued for their reproductive capacity to the occlusion of their other abilities. In another sense, however, they were undervalued, with the uterus seen as a passive receptacle for the "active" male seed. (In patrilineal societies, this view did make good sense as a biological parallel to the kinship structure in which women's offspring belonged to the male lineage.)

Romans 8, however, redefines the contracting uterus of a laboring woman as a metaphor for hope: "the whole creation has been groaning in labor pains until now; and not only the creation, but we ourselves, who have the first fruits of the Spirit, groan inwardly while we wait for adoption, the redemption of our bodies" (Romans 8:22-23 NRSV). It's a mixed metaphor, with more than one meaning. On the one hand readers are encouraged to remember, each time a woman labors, that we and all of creation are struggling toward birth; suffering is not for nothing. On the other hand, however, readers are reminded that these labor pains lead to adoption, which is the dominant metaphor for inclusion in God's family—not biological family.

Thus, there are two renewed meanings: First, women's reproductive capacity is not simply a passive, sideline pursuit that contributes to a man's lineage. Labor and delivery are exciting, active processes that help us picture what suffering and redemption mean on a much larger scale. Second, just as the Jews were not to value circumcision of the body over circumcision of the heart, neither should we mistake biological relatedness as the best metaphor for God's family. Both circumcision and biological reproduction encourage people to prioritize ethnic belonging over spiritual family, when in reality, adoption into God's family is the real deal.

Similar to the Jews' view of circumcision, the pattern of the world today is to treat sexual desire as a "flag" for human identity; it alerts us to who a person really is. The sexual identity framework invites people to publicly assert the direction of their sexual feelings and claim social, political and religious solidarity with others who have similar sexual feelings. Showcasing sexuality in this way is an immodest presentation of an "unpresentable" part. We could make more of sexuality, that is, show it greater honor, by making less of sexual desire.

The invitation for us is to assign new meaning to the direction of sexual feelings. If wanting to have sex with a particular person, or a particular type of person, isn't an indicator of identity, then what do those feelings mean? Like Paul's redefinition of foreskin, we could redefine sexual desire as simply a part—not the whole—of who we are. Neither foreskin nor sexual desire should be used as a public marker of identity and a criterion around which to establish groups of insiders and outsiders. Moreover, sexual desire could, like the uterus, become a lens through which we see greater spiritual insight, instead of being an element of life that circumscribes a person's worth and social role. Perhaps in our sexual histories and current states, we can view bigger pictures of grace, mercy, sin, repentance or redemption.

Mutual Affection and Greater Honor

In many corporate contexts, such as denominations, state and national politics, and media discourse, the sexual identity framework and its fixed-position debates are entrenched. Beginning to cultivate discernment, repentance and respectful conversation can have profound consequences in corporate contexts, but it will likely not happen quickly or easily. We didn't create the tensions and conundrums around same-sex sexuality that are damaging Christian churches, denominations, families and other communities; we inherited them. The sexual identity framework, and the theological debates it has spawned, is a hundred years old, and it came on the heels of centuries of discomfort and disagreement about sexuality within Christianity. Seen in another light, however, the sexual identity framework is *only* a hundred years old; it hasn't always existed, and it won't always exist. Disagreements about sexual ethics, as well as divergent sexual practices among Christians, will surely remain long after the sexual identity framework passes away, but perhaps we can begin holding those differences within the body instead of lopping off the parts we find disagreeable.

Driven by genuine love, people are making their way around, under, over and through the sexual identity impasse. A son comes out as gay, and while his parents can't give him the theological affirmation he desires, they somehow continue to fully love each other. A Christian college allows its faculty to hold divergent viewpoints about homosexuality (at many Christian colleges, faculty cannot theologically affirm same-sex intimacy), and while some backbite and/or avoid each other, others seek out dialogue and friendship with those who hold different views. In small groups and friendships, people talk about their sexual feelings, choices and relationships with true vulnerability and openness to feedback without prepackaging their sexuality with labels that ratchet the stakes up to the level of identity. When disagreements about same-sex sexuality are just differences, not divisions, and when we share mutual affection and bestow honor on those with whom we disagree, we're already living beyond the end of sexual identity.

Discussion Questions

Preface

1. Is there an experience or relationship in your life that has raised significant issues for you related to sexual identity? If so, what are the lingering questions, and what do they mean to you now?

Introduction: A Word About Sex

1. In your experience with Christians or in Christian settings, how has the topic of sex been handled? Are there ways in which Christians have made too big a deal of sex? Are there ways in which Christians should make an even bigger deal of sex?

2. How do you respond to sexual content in society? How should Christians engage culture?

3. Tell a story about a time when you observed or participated in respectful conversation about sexuality. What are some of the characteristics of respectful conversation?

Chapter One: What Is Defined as Real

1. Have you ever visited or lived in a society where sex and/or gender were very different than in your home culture? Describe the differences and what you learned from the experience.

2. How do you respond to the notion that sexual identity is a social construction? Is this a new idea or a familiar one? How could it change the way you view others? How could it change the way you view yourself?

3. In your opinion, which elements of your society's sex, gender or sexuality categories pattern God's creation well? Which elements miss the mark? By what criteria do you make these distinctions?

Chapter Two: The Trouble with Heterosexuality

1. What are some of the symbols (dress, speech, movement, behaviors, etc.) that people use to express heterosexuality? Are these symbols different in various contexts or time periods?

2. What could it mean, in your context, to betray heterosexuality? Are there practical ways that you could ignore, minimize or strategically engage heterosexuality, instead of taking it for granted as a necessary way of viewing people?

3. How important are sexual identity categories in your own self-understanding? What other dimensions of life (sex, gender, religion, life stage, etc.) influence how you view and live out your sexuality?

4. What are some ways that the concept of heterosexuality causes problems in Christian communities? Are there ways in which it is beneficial?

Chapter Three: The Trouble with Homosexuality

1. What are the most common words (*gay, lesbian, LGBTQ, homosexual,* etc.) used to describe sexual minorities in your communities? What is useful about those concepts, and what are their limitations?

2. How do you respond to the notion that same-sex sex takes a variety of patterns around the world? How does this shape how you view your own society?

3. What do you think of unlabeled sexuality? Do you know any people who refuse to label their sexuality? What are their reasons for doing so?

Chapter Four: The Promise of Sexual Holiness

1. Practice "unpacking the groceries." What are some of the important elements of human sexuality, the items in the bags? Make as long a list as you can.

2. How do you define holiness? How does this chapter confirm, challenge or add to your understanding?

3. Choose one of the dimensions of holiness and use it to interpret or evaluate a situation related to sexual identity that you've heard about, read about or experienced.

4. What do you think of a weaned child in its mother's lap as a picture of a person in relationship with God? Would this image describe how people deal with sexual issues in Christian communities or churches you know?

Chapter Five: Sexual Desire Is (Not) a Big Deal

1. How would you describe the connection between sexual desire and human identity? How does this chapter confirm, challenge or add to your understanding?

2. What are some differences between judgment and discernment? How could discernment benefit Christians as they deal with human sexuality?

3. What are some dangers in attempting to "cure" same-sex desire? What might it mean for people to care for their sexuality instead of trying to cure it?

Chapter Six: Having Sex Is (Not) a Big Deal

1. What are some of the myths about marriage and sex that you have heard in Christian contexts? What are some valuable truths you've learned, and in what contexts did you learn them?

2. How could the Hebrew concept of *yada* renew or extend common understandings of sex in your society?

3. How could the metaphor of marriage as a crucible influence how you view sex within marriage as well as sex outside of marriage?

Chapter Seven: Celibacy Is (Not) a Big Deal

1. What are some everyday ways in which churches and other Christian communities make celibacy seem both implausible and impractical? What are some solutions—practices that support the idea of celibacy as well as the people who live it out?

2. Do you know any self-actualized celibates (or are you one)? What are some of the qualities that characterize celibacy at its best?

Epilogue: The End Is Near

1. Do you believe the end of sexuality identity is a good thing? Why or why not?

2. Give an example of a relationship, conversation, behavior or other specific instance of Christians moving beyond the sexual identity framework.

Notes

Introduction

[1]Planned Parenthood, "Health Topics" <www.plannedparenthood.org/health-topics/birth-control/outercourse-4371.htm>.

[2]Here and throughout, my perspective on Romans 12 is shaped by Michael R. Cosby, *Apostle on the Edge: An Inductive Approach to Paul* (Louisville: Westminster John Knox, 2009); Craig Keener, *The IVP Bible Background Commentary: New Testament* (Downers Grove, Ill.: InterVarsity Press, 1993); Douglas J. Moo, *The Epistle to the Romans* (Grand Rapids: Eerdmans, 1996).

[3]American Anthropological Association, AAA Code of Ethics <www.aaanet.org/committees/ethics/ethicscode.pdf>.

[4]See Jean Kilbourne's website at <www.jeankilbourne.com>.

[5]Andy Crouch, *Culture Making: Recovering Our Creative Calling* (Downers Grove, Ill.: IVP Books, 2008).

[6]See Harold Heie, *Learning to Listen, Ready to Talk: A Pilgrimage Toward Peacemaking* (Lincoln, Nebr.: iUniverse, 2007).

Chapter One: What Is Defined as Real

[1]Known as the Thomas theorem, this was published in William I. Thomas and Dorothy Swaine Thomas, *The Child in America: Behavior Problems and Programs* (New York: Alfred A. Knopf, 1928), pp. 571-72. I paraphrased the original with gender-inclusive language.

[2]Sharyn Graham Davies, *Challenging Gender Norms: Five Genders Among Bugis in Indonesia* (Belmont, Calif.: Thomson Wadsworth, 2007). For more on the social construction of gender, see Judith Butler, *Undoing Gender* (New York: Routledge, 2004); Serena Nanda, *Gender Diversity: Crosscultural Variations* (Prospect Heights, Ill.: Waveland, 2000).

[3]I have generalized Bugis culture for brevity's sake. Their culture is internally diverse; in some regions, Davies found people who conceptualized

gender in different ways, and her book describes this variety in detail. See also Sharyn Graham, "It's Like One of Those Puzzles: Conceptualising Gender Among Bugis," *Journal of Gender Studies* 13, no. 2 (2004): 107-16.

[4]Judith Butler, *Undoing Gender* (New York: Routledge, 2004), p. 10.

[5]For more on a Christian perspective of social construction, see Peter Berger, *The Sacred Canopy: Elements of a Sociological Theory of Religion* (1967; reprint, New York: Anchor Books, 1990).

Chapter Two: The Trouble with Heterosexuality

[1]Anthropologists have documented the histories of sexual minority communities in various U.S. locations. See Brett Beemyn, *Creating a Place for Ourselves: Lesbian, Gay and Bisexual Community Histories* (New York: Routledge, 1997); Lillian Faderman, *Odd Girls and Twilight Lovers: A History of Lesbian Life in Twentieth-Century America* (New York: Penguin Group, 1991); Elizabeth Lapovsky Kennedy and Madeline D. Davis, *Boots of Leather, Slippers of Gold: The History of a Lesbian Community* (New York: Penguin, 1993).

[2]Jonathan Ned Katz, "'Homosexual' and 'Heterosexual': Questioning the Terms," in *A Queer World: The Center for Lesbian and Gay Studies Reader,* ed. Martin Duberman (New York: New York University Press, 1997).

[3]John D'Emilio and Estelle B. Freedman, *Intimate Matters: A History of Sexuality in America* (Chicago: University of Chicago Press, 1997).

[4]Ibid., pp. 4-38.

[5]Katz, "'Homosexual' and 'Heterosexual'"; Jonathan Ned Katz, *The Invention of Heterosexuality* (New York: Dutton, 1959).

[6]Alfred Kinsey, Wardell B. Pomeroy and Clyde E. Martin, *Sexual Behavior in the Human Male* (Philadelphia: W. B. Saunders, 1948), p. 639.

[7]Ibid., p. 638.

[8]Fritz Klein, *The Bisexual Option*, 2nd ed. (1978; reprint, Binghamton, N.Y.: Haworth, 1993).

[9]Roy F. Baumeister, "Gender Differences in Erotic Plasticity: The Female Sex Drive as Socially Flexible and Responsive," *Psychological Bulletin* 126, no. 3 (2000): 347-74.

[10]Edward O. Laumann, John Gagnon, Robert Michael and Stuart Michaels, *The Social Organization of Sexuality: Sexual Practices in the United States* (Chicago: University of Chicago Press, 1994).

[11]Mark Regnerus, *Forbidden Fruit: Sex and Religion in the Lives of American Teenagers* (New York: Oxford University Press, 2007), p. 77. This data was derived from the National Survey of Family Growth, Cycle 6.

[12]Michael Kimmel, *The Gendered Society,* 3rd ed. (New York: Oxford Uni-

versity Press, 2008); Elline Lipkin, *Girls' Studies* (Berkeley, Calif.: Seal, 2009).

[13]Crystal Downing, "God Savor *The Queen*," *Books & Culture* 14 (November/December 2008): 24-25.

[14]R. T. France, *Matthew* (Grand Rapids: Eerdmans, 1985), pp. 253-54.

Chapter Three: The Trouble with Homosexuality

[1]Edward O. Laumann, John Gagnon, Robert Michael and Stuart Michaels, *The Social Organization of Sexuality: Sexual Practices in the United States* (Chicago: University of Chicago Press, 1994), p. 299.

[2]Ibid., p. 299.

[3]Michel Foucault, *The History of Sexuality: An Introduction*, Vintage ed. (1978; reprint, New York: Random House, 1990).

[4]Garret Keizer, "Turning Away from Jesus: Gay Rights and the War for the Episcopal Church," *Harper's Magazine* 316 (June 2008): 39-50.

[5]Brian Mustanski, Meredith Chivers and J. Michael Bailey, "A Critical Review of Recent Biological Research on Human Sexual Orientation," *Annual Review of Sex Research* 13 (2002): 89-139; Letitia Anne Peplau, Leah Spalding, Terri Conley and Rosemary Veniegas, "The Development of Sexual Orientation in Women," *Annual Review of Sex Research* 10 (1999): 70-99; Paula Rodriguez Rust, "Bisexuality: The State of the Union," *Annual Review of Sex Research* 13 (2002): 180-240. For Christian perspective on scientific research, see Stanton Jones, *Homosexuality: The Use of Scientific Research in the Church's Moral Debate* (Downers Grove, Ill.: InterVarsity Press, 2000).

[6]Pat Caplan, "Introduction," in *The Cultural Construction of Sexuality,* ed. Pat Caplan (London: Routledge, 1987), p. 25.

[7]David Greenberg, *The Construction of Homosexuality* (Chicago: University of Chicago Press, 1988); Gil Herdt, ed., *Third Sex, Third Gender: Beyond Sexual Dimorphism in Culture and History* (New York: Zone Books, 1994); Stephen Murray, *Homosexualities* (Chicago: University of Chicago Press, 2000).

[8]Murray, *Homosexualities*, pp. 25-71, 204-10.

[9]Evelyn Blackwood, "Culture and Women's Sexualities," *Journal of Social Issues* 56, no. 2 (2000): 223-38.

[10]Greenberg, *Construction of Homosexuality*, pp. 152-63.

[11]James Neill, *The Origins and Role of Same-Sex Relations in Human Societies* (Jefferson, N.C.: McFarland, 2009).

[12]Carlos F. Caceres and Ana Maria Rosasco, "The Margin Has Many Sides: Diversity Among Gay and Homosexually Active Men in Lima," *Culture,*

Health and Sexuality 1, no. 3 (1999): 261-75.

[13]Lee Wallace, "*Fa'afafine: Queens of Samoa* and the Elision of Homosexuality," *GLQ: A Journal of Lesbian and Gay Studies* 5, no. 1 (1999): 25-40.

[14]Lillian Faderman, Odd Girls and Twilight Lovers: A History of Lesbian Life in Twentieth-Century America (New York: Penguin, 1991).

[15]Stephen O. Murray, *Pacific Homosexualities* (Lincoln, Nebr.: Writers Club, 2002), pp. 348-53.

[16]Sharyn Graham Davies, *Challenging Gender Norms: Five Genders Among Bugis in Indonesia* (Belmont, Calif.: Thomson Wadsworth, 2007).

[17]See examples in Murray, *Homosexualities*, pp. 357-81.

[18]Jeffrey Weeks, "Questions of Identity," in *The Cultural Construction of Sexuality*, ed. Pat Caplan (London: Routledge, 1987), p. 42.

[19]Mindy Michels and Jenell Williams, "'Finding Common Ground': Anti-Gay Violence and Public Discourse," *The Graduate Review* (American University) (1996): 18-27.

[20]Jenell Williams Paris and Rory Anderson, "Faith-Based Queer Space in Washington, D.C.: The Metropolitan Community Church–D.C. and Mount Vernon Square," *Gender, Place and Culture* 8, no. 2 (2001): 149-68.

[21]Shaka McGlotten, "Blackness and Queer Speculations," *Anthropology News* 50, no. 7 (October 2009): 48-49.

[22]Rebecca F. Plante, *Sexualities in Context: A Social Perspective* (New York: Westview, 2006).

[23]Kelly Brooks and Kathryn Quina, "Women's Sexual Identity Patterns: Differences Among Lesbians, Bisexuals, and Unlabeled Women," *Journal of Homosexuality* 56, no. 8 (2009): 1030-45.

[24]Lisa M. Diamond, *Sexual Fluidity: Understanding Women's Love and Desire* (Cambridge, Mass.: Harvard University Press), pp. 61-65.

[25]Mark Yarhouse, Stephen Stratton, Janet Dean and Heather Brooke, "Listening to Sexual Minorities on Christian College Campuses," *Journal of Psychology and Theology* 37, no. 2 (2009): 96-113.

[26]McGlotten, "Blackness and Queer Speculations," pp. 48-49.

Chapter Four: The Promise of Sexual Holiness

[1]Mildred Wynkoop, *A Theology of Love: The Dynamic of Wesleyanism* (Kansas City, Mo.: Beacon Hill, 1972), p. 158.

[2]Kevin W. Mannoia and Don Thorsen, eds., *The Holiness Manifesto* (Grand Rapids: Eerdmans, 2008). Churches included Church of the Nazarene, Free Methodist Church, the Salvation Army, Church of God (Anderson), Shield of Faith, Brethren in Christ, Evangelical Friends, Church of God in Christ, International Church of the Foursquare Gospel, Christian and Mis-

sionary Alliance and International Pentecostal Holiness.

[3]Biblical research that has shaped my view includes Richard Davidson, *Flame of Yahweh: Sexuality in the Old Testament* (Peabody, Mass.: Hendrickson, 2007); Robert Gagnon, *The Bible and Homosexual Practice: Texts and Hermeneutics* (Nashville: Abingdon, 2001); Donald Wold, *Out of Order: Homosexuality in the Bible and the Ancient Near East* (Grand Rapids: Baker, 1998).

[4]See International Justice Mission's website at <www.ijm.org>.

[5]Kathryn Joyce, *Quiverfull: Inside the Christian Patriarchy Movement* (Boston: Beacon, 2009). See also God's Word to Women, the ministry of Catherine Clark Kroeger that addresses domestic abuse in Christian homes: <www.godswordtowomen.org/kroeger.htm>.

[6]Mannoia and Thorsen, *Holiness Manifesto*, p. 22.

[7]Debra W. Haffner and Timothy Palmer, *Sexuality and Religion 2020: Goals for the Next Decade* (Westport, Conn.: Religious Institute, 2010), p.10.

[8]Dietrich Bonhoeffer, *The Cost of Discipleship* (1937; reprint, New York: Touchstone, 1995), p. 45.

[9]For more on this idea, see Gregory Boyd, *Repenting of Religion: Turning from Judgment to the Love of God* (Grand Rapids: Baker, 2004).

Chapter Five: Sexual Desire Is (Not) A Big Deal

[1]Elizabeth Moberly, *Homosexuality: A New Christian Ethic* (Cambridge, England: James Clarke, 1983).

[2]Jeanette Howard, *Into the Promised Land: Beyond the Lesbian Struggle* (Grand Rapids: Kregel, 2005), pp. 9-10.

[3]Stanton L. Jones and Mark A. Yarhouse, *Ex-Gays? A Longitudinal Study of Religiously Mediated Change in Sexual Orientation* (Downers Grove, Ill.: InterVarsity Press, 2007). The results are based on seventy-eight people (of the original ninety-eight) and are discussed at length in chapter eight. See also Stanton L. Jones and Mark Yarhouse, "Ex Gays? An Extended Longitudinal Study of Attempted Religiously Mediated Change in Sexual Orientation," Sexual Orientation and Faith Tradition Symposium, APA Convention, 2009.

[4]Mark Yarhouse, "Note from the Director," *Institute for the Study of Sexual Identity Update* 8 (November/December 2009): 1.

[5]Edward O. Laumann, John Gagnon, Robert Michael and Stuart Michaels, *The Social Organization of Sexuality: Sexual Practices in the United States* (Chicago: University of Chicago Press, 1994), p. 290.

[6]Lisa M. Diamond, *Sexual Fluidity: Understanding Women's Love and Desire* (Cambridge, Mass.: Harvard University Press, 2008).

[7]Roy F. Baumeister, "Gender Differences in Erotic Plasticity: The Female Sex Drive as Socially Flexible and Responsive," *Psychological Bulletin* 126, no. 3 (2000): 347-74.

[8]Metropolitan Community Churches, "MCC Statement of Purpose" <www .mccchurch.org/mediaroom/presskit/purpose.pdf>.

[9]See Warren Throckmorton's website and blog at <www.drthrockmorton. com>. Also see the website for the Institute for the Study of Sexual Identity, where Mark Yarhouse is the executive director, at <www.sexualidentityin-stitute.org>.

[10]Thomas Moore, *Care of the Soul: A Guide for Cultivating Depth and Sacredness in Everyday Life* (New York: HarperCollins, 1992), p. 18.

[11]Tanya Erzen, *Straight to Jesus: Sexual and Christian Conversions in the Ex-Gay Movement* (Berkeley: University of California Press, 2006).

[12]Ibid., pp. 218-19.

[13]Howard, *Into the Promised Land,* p. 65.

Chapter Six: Having Sex Is (Not) a Big Deal

[1]Jenell Williams Paris, "The Truth About Sex," *Christianity Today* 45, no. 14 (2001): 62-64.

[2]*Strong's Concordance* at <www.blueletterbible.org/lang/lexicon/lexicon .cfm?Strongs=H3045&t=KJV>; G. Johannes Botterweck and Helmer Ringgren, *Theological Dictionary of the Old Testament* (Grand Rapids: Eerdmans, 1974-1975).

[3]Steven Garber, *The Fabric of Faithfulness: Weaving Together Belief and Behavior,* exp. ed. (Downers Grove, Ill.: InterVarsity Press, 2007).

[4]Mildred Wynkoop, *A Theology of Love: The Dynamic of Wesleyanism* (Kansas City, Mo.: Beacon Hill, 1972), pp. 27-31.

[5]Michael R. Cosby, *Sex in the Bible: An Introduction to What the Scriptures Teach Us About Sexuality* (Englewood Cliffs, N.J.: Prentice-Hall, 1984), p. 84.

Chapter Seven: Celibacy Is (Not) a Big Deal

[1]Peter S. Bearman and Hannah Brückner, "Promising the Future: Virginity Pledges and First Intercourse," *American Journal of Sociology* 106 (2001): 859-912. For more on religion and teen sexuality, see Mark Regnerus, *Forbidden Fruit: Sex and Religion in the Lives of American Teenagers* (New York: Oxford University Press, 2007).

[2]Stanton L. Jones and Mark A. Yarhouse, *Ex-Gays? A Longitudinal Study of Religiously Mediated Change in Sexual Orientation* (Downers Grove, Ill.: InterVarsity Press, 2007).

[3]Mark Regnerus, "The Case for Early Marriage," *Christianity Today* 53, no. 8 (August 2009): 22-28. For more on Christian celibacy, see Christine A. Colón and Bonnie E. Field, *Singled Out: Why Celibacy Must Be Reinvented in Today's Church* (Grand Rapids: Brazos, 2009).

[4]Donald Wold, *Out of Order: Homosexuality in the Bible and the Ancient Near East* (Grand Rapids: Baker, 1998).

[5]Peter Berger, The Sacred Canopy: Elements of a Sociological Theory of Religion (1967; reprint, New York: Anchor Books, 1990).

[6]Elisa J. Sobo and Sandra Bell, eds., *Celibacy, Culture and Society: The Anthropology of Sexual Abstinence* (Madison: University of Wisconsin Press, 2001).

[7]Denise Donnelly, Elisabeth Burgess, Sally Anderson, Regina Davis and Joy Dillard, "Involuntary Celibacy: A Life Course Analysis," *The Journal of Sex Research* 38, no. 2 (2001): 159-69.

[8]Anne M. Hoenkamp-Bisschops, "Catholic Priests and Their Experience of Celibacy," *Journal of Religion and Health* 31, no. 4 (1992): 327-36.

[9]Dayna Olson-Getty, "The Witness of Celibate Sexuality: A Challenge to Evangelical Theology and Practice of Single Sexuality," unpublished paper, InterVarsity Ministry Exchange <www.intervarsity.org/mx/item/3831/>, p. 10.

[10]Gerdenio M. Manuel, "Religious Celibacy from the Celibate's Point of View," *Journal of Religion and Health* 28, no. 4 (1989): 279-97.

[11]Kathleen Norris, *Amazing Grace: A Vocabulary of Faith* (New York: Riverhead Books, 1998), p. 263.

[12]Olson-Getty, "Witness of Celibate Sexuality," p. 6.

[13]"Let Your Sins Be Strong: A Letter from Luther to Melanchthon," accessed at <www.iclnet.org/pub/resources/text/wittenberg/luther/letsinsbe.txt>.

Acknowledgments

I am indebted to a great number of people whose friendship, support and critique were vital for the completion of this book. After delivering a series of talks on sexuality at George Fox University, H. David Brandt, the president at the time, encouraged me to write this book, one of several projects that has benefited from his enthusiasm. At Bethel University, where my writing began, I'm grateful for support from students and colleagues including Jay Barnes, Curtiss DeYoung, Jim Hurd, Lindsay Johnson, Bamidele Andrew Odubote, Harley Schreck and Samuel Zalanga. Minnesota friends who never tired of talking about sexuality with me included Rachel Anderson, Victor Barge, Carla Barnhill, Jimmy Barnhill, Kathryn Green, Katie Hutton, Shelley Pagitt, Naomi Schwenke and Colleen Welch.

I finished the book at Messiah College, where I'm thankful for support from colleagues, including Gene Chase, Michael Cosby, Kris Hansen-Kieffer, Dean Susan Hasseler, Meg Hoover, Douglas (Jake) Jacobsen, Rhonda Jacobsen, Faith Minnich, President Kim Phipps, Susie Stanley, Brian Smith and Amy VanDerWerf. Messiah College librarians Beth Transue and Liz Kielley always helped me find what I needed, and Beth offered valuable manuscript critique as well. The Pinklings, my writer's group, struck the right balance between incisive critique, lavish encouragement and good dessert. Pinklings include Sharon Baker, Lynne Cosby, Crystal Downing, Meg Ramey, Valerie Smith, Valerie Weaver-Zercher and Cynthia

Wells. Students who read, critiqued and/or edited the manuscript include Karli Davis, Caitlin Kruse, Chelsea McIntyre, Kate Miller, Samantha Moore, Ben Olsen, John Sommerville, and students in the fall 2008 Sexuality in Cross-Cultural Perspective class and the spring 2010 Women and Men in American Society class.

Blog readers provided essential critique via email and comments; thanks especially to Andrea Allen, Troy Blomquist, Randy Hughes, Christy Lambertson, Karen Maezen Miller, Heidi Renee, John Schaefer, Hugo Schwyzer and Ben Williams. I also relied on expert perspective from Mark Regnerus, Warren Throckmorton and Megan DeFranza.

I'm very grateful to Al Hsu, my editor at IVP, for seeing through a rough draft to the book it could become.

I often wanted more time alone to write, but even more than that, I didn't want to miss or be missed by my family. Thanks to Oliver (four), Wesley (four) and Maxwell (three), for being so crazy and so adorable. Thanks to Ian, Simon and Gordon, my triplets who passed away at birth, for having come to me. And thanks to James, my husband, for believing in me and (most of) my ideas.

Name and Subject Index

activo-pasivo, 66
Adam and Eve,
91-92, 115-16
additive
    approaches to
    sexual identity
    labels, 72, 74
adultery, 42
age-structured
    same-sex
    relationships,
    63, 64-66
alphabetic
    approaches to
    sexual identity
    labels, 72, 74
    LGBT, 72
    LGBTQ, 72
    LGBTQQI, 72
    LGBTQQPA
    (H),BDSM,
    72
American
    Anthropological
    Association,
    17-18
American
    Psychological
    Association, 102
American Studies
    Program, 18,
    115
Anderson, Rory,
    72
anthropology, 59
    definition, 15,
    16-18
    social
    construc-

tion, 8
arsenokoites, 64
Baumeister, Roy,
    46, 104
beauty, 140
beloved, 96-99
Bethel University,
    18-19
biology, 59, 62
bisexuality, 46
bissu, 26-29
Bonhoeffer,
    Dietrich, 87
Borneo, 67
Bugis, 26-29, 60,
    67, 69
butch-femme, 67
Butler, Judith, 33
calabai, 26-29, 60
calalai, 26-29, 60
Caplan, Pat, 61
Caribbean, 66
Catholic (Roman),
    130, 133
celibacy, 126-38
    in crosscultural
    perspective,
    130
circumcision,
    141-43
Cosby, Michael,
    119
Crouch, Andy, 21
crucible, marriage
    as a, 117-22
culture
    Christians and,
    13
    and religion,

29, 36, 52
Dahomey (Benin),
    68
Davies, Bob, 108,
    110
Davies, Sharyn
    Graham, 26
Diamond, Lisa
    M., 73, 103-4
discernment, 106
Donnelly, Dense,
    132-33
Downing,
    Crystal, 50
egalitarian
    same-sex
    relationships,
    63, 68-69
Erzen, Tanya, 108
ethics, 17
ex-gay, 55, 70, 108
Exodus Interna-
    tional, 108
fa-afafine, 66-67
fixed-position
    debate, 21, 27
fornication, 42
Gagnon, John,
    56-57
Garber, Steve, 115
gender
    definition,
    31-35
    gender-struc-
    tured
    same-sex
    relationships,
    63, 66-67
    identity, 42

nonconformity,
    69
    roles, 48-49
genetics, 60, 62
GPA, 51-52, 84
Greece, 64-65,
    68-69
grocery bags,
    79-82
Heie, Harold, 21
Herskovits,
    Melville, 68
heterosexuality, 9
    betraying,
    50-52
    biblical
    problem
    with, 43-44
    definition of,
    30, 39
    performance
    of, 48
    practical
    problem
    with, 48-50
    scientific
    problem
    with, 44-48
Hindmarsh,
    Bruce, 10
Hinduism, 130
Hoenkamp-Biss-
    chop, Anne, 133
homosexuality
    difficulty of
    defining, 30,
    55-57
    history of,
    57-60

origins of, 60-62

and sin, 34

Howard, Jeanette, 100, 108

International Justice Mission, 85

intersex, 28, 31

invert, 40

Islam (Muslim), 26, 28

Jones, Stanton, 100-102, 108

Keizer, Garret, 59

Kilbourne, Jean, 20

Kinsey, Alfred, 44

Kinsey Reports, 44-45

Kinsey Scale, 45

Klein Sexual Orientation Grid, 46-47

Latin America, 69

Laumann, Edward, 46, 56-57

LGBTQ, 62, 63, and public discourse, 70-71

Luther, Martin, 136

malakos, 64-65

Manuel, Gerdenio, 134

marriage, 111-15

masturbation, 42

McGlotten, Shaka, 72, 74

Melanesia, 11

mental hygiene, 63

Mediterranean, 66

Messiah College, 18-19, 21

Mesoamerica, 66

Metropolitan Community Church (MCC), 72, 105-6

Michael, Robert, 56-57

Michaels, Stuart, 56-57

Michels, Mindy, 70

Moberly, Elizabeth, 100

Moore, Thomas, 108

Murray, Stephen, 63

National Health and Social Life Study, 56-57

Native America (Native Americans), 67, 69

New Hope Ministries, 108

niceness, 19

Norris, Kathleen, 134

Nuer, 61

nursing, 77-78, 91

Olson-Getty, Dayna, 134

oral sex, 13

othering (sexual others), 70-71

outercourse, 10

Philadelphia (the film), 128

Philippines, 67

plausibility structure, 129-31

Point Loma Nazarene University, 20

profession-based same-sex relationships, 63, 67-68

psychology, 59-60, 62

queer, 72

Regenerus, Mark, 48

reparative therapy, 100-102

repentance, 104

romantic ideal, 111-12

Rome (Roman), 65, 68

Samoa, 66-67, 69

self-actualized celibates, 134-35

Sermon on the Mount, 118

sex (sexuality) as a continuum, 44-45

and culture, 21

definition and purpose, 10-12, 31

potentially offensive content, 20

unlabeled, 53, 72-74

sexual desire, 97-105

sexual dimorphism, 31

sexual fluidity (erotic plasticity), 46, 102-4

sexual fulfillment, 112-15

sexual holiness, 13, 16, 82-83

blessing and suffering, 89, 117

Christ-centered and Holy Spirit-centered, 86-87

in community, 90-92

crisis and process, 88-89

development and end, 87-88

dimensions of, 84

as framework, 82-83

individual and corporate, 84-86

and morality, 83

separation and incarnation, 89-90

sexual identity categories, 57

as part of culture, 25

sexual identity

framework, 41
origins of,
    41-42
and sexual
    desire, 93-96
weaning from,
    78
Shaker Christians,
    130
Siberia, 67
social construc-
    tion, 8-9, 75
    of heterosexu-

ality, 41-44
    of sex
    categories,
    31-34
sodomy (sod-
    omite), 42, 57,
    61
South America,
    66
South Sulawesi,
    26-29
Thailand, 91
Throckmorton,

Warren, 106
tribad, 40
two-spirit
    (berdache), 67
Uganda, 59
unchaste church,
    131-32
urning, 40
values coherence,
    106
weaning, 77-78,
    91
Weeks, Jeffrey, 70

Wesley, John, 83,
    105, 137
Wold, Donald,
    127
Worthen, Frank
    and Anita, 108
Wynkoop,
    Mildred, 83, 118
yada, 115-16
Yarhouse, Mark,
    73, 100-102,
    106, 108

Scripture Index

Genesis
1:27, *31-32,*
    96-97
2:19, *35*
4:1-2, *115*
34, *97*

Leviticus
18, *88*
20, *88*

Deuteronomy
30:6, *141*

2 Samuel
11, *97*

Psalms
131, *77, 79*
145:16, *98*

Song of Solomon
7:10, *98*

Isaiah
43:1, *97*

Jeremiah
17:9-10, *43*

Matthew
5:27-30, *118*
9:12, *107*
9:36, *97*
11:30, *126*
16:13-16, *52-53*
22:34-40,
    83

Mark
1:15, *104*

Luke
1:37, *126*

John
8:1-11, *118-22*

Romans
1, *88*
2:3-4, *120*
2:24, *120*
2:29, *141*
7:18, *98, 99*
8:22-23, *142*
12, *14-15, 25, 105*
12:1-2, *40, 90,
    122*
12:3, *40, 80*
12:4-10, *139*

1 Corinthians
6, *88*
6:9, *64*
7:7, *138*
12:22-25, *141*

2 Corinthians
12:1-10, *137, 141*
12:9-10, *109*

Galatians
5:22-23, *117*

Philippians
2:13, *98*
3:19, *63*

1 Timothy
1, *88*
1:10, *64*
2:11, *86*

2 Timothy
3:5, *105*

Hebrews
11:13-14, *129-30*

James
1:14-15, *97*